Praise for *Securely*

Children grow, develop, and learn in the c
on lessons learned through lived experienc
Kristin and Mike Berry—with humor, truth-telling, and insight—bring
this important message to parents and caregivers of all stripes. I highly
recommend this book to all foster and adoptive parents who find themselves in the middle of the night asking, "What do I do now?"

IRA J. CHASNOFF, MD, President, NTI Upstream; professor of Clinical
Pediatrics, University of Illinois College of Medicine

I want this book put in the hands of all adoptive parents who are not
already experts in developmental trauma. Even those who have heard this
information before can appreciate the relatable voice with which the Berrys
teach. Mike and Kristin are wonderful, quiet leaders and knowledgeable
teachers. This book shares beautiful, understandable examples. Readers will
feel understood, informed, and empowered to parent through trauma with
love.

BROOKE RANDOLPH, LMHC, Founder & Director, Counseling at The
Green House; Certified Brainspotting Therapist & Consultant; Certified
Imago Relationship Therapist

Mike and Kristin Berry's new book, *Securely Attached*, is an engaging conversation between the Berrys and their readers. The Berrys coach adoptive
and foster parents, giving examples, scripts, and information in a format
that answers typical questions: "Why do they do that?" and "What should
I do?" The practical advice in the book runs the gamut of parenting experiences, from an observation checklist to pin down the source of a child's
dysregulation, to how to form a safety plan for a child/teen who poses
a danger to others. In one of my favorite chapters, the authors describe
the "floors" of a child/teen's brain, and how to react accordingly. *Securely
Attached* succeeds in providing straightforward explanations for complex
issues. The authors provide plans to reduce the challenges to attachment—
trauma, sensory issues, losses, and behaviors. Every reader who is parenting
through adoption, guardianship, or foster care will find new methods and
insights in this book. Best of all, they will experience the Berrys cheering
for their families.

DEBORAH D. GRAY, LICSW, author of *Promoting Healthy Attachments*;
Attaching Through Love, Hugs, and Play; *Attaching in Adoption*; and *Nurtur-
ing Adoptions*; coauthor of *Games and Activities for Attaching with Your Child*

Securely Attached is for every foster and/or adoptive parent. Mike and Kristin have bravely taken the science of trauma and attachment and coupled it with real-life examples, based on their years of personal experience, and made a complete resource full of practical insight. While there are a number of books I recommend to foster and adoptive families, *Securely Attached* will now be my go-to resource because it presents the information, examples, and applications all in one place. This is a book that I think parents will refer to over and over again.

JEN DECKER, founder and director, the RE:Conference for foster and adoptive parents

This book is for all parents with children who have experienced trauma, neglect, and/or have been exposed to drugs and alcohol before birth. This will be an inspiration to parents who are desperately seeking answers to really challenging parenting situations. Mike and Kristin share their rich, relatable, and practical insights. This book is full of parenting wisdom! It is a must-read!

GARY FELDMAN, MD, Medical Director of Stramski Children's Developmental Center at Miller Children's & Women's Hospital, Long Beach, CA

Understanding the impact of early childhood trauma changes everything. It changes how we see ourselves, our children, and the people around us. Mike and Kristin Berry, adoptive parents of eight children, have handed us an amazing lens from which to view the life of those adults and children who have come through early-life traumatic experiences. Understanding the impact of trauma is one thing. Knowing how to navigate through the challenges and needs of children to lead them to healing is quite another. The Berrys have given us both—understanding and the how-to—in this remarkable book, based on solid scientific grounding and their own life experiences. This would make a great book club study for foster and adoptive parents. I highly recommend this book.

JAYNE E. SCHOOLER, Director of Affiliate Training, Trauma Free World; author of *Wounded Children, Healing Homes: How Traumatized Children Impact Adoptive and Foster Families*

Mike and Kristin don't just talk the talk, they walk the walk day in and day out with their own marvelously diverse adoptive family. In a way that combines knowledge, heart, truth, and grace they break down complex trauma and attachment concepts in a way that is both accessible to parents and supported by stories of their own parenting experiences. Whether you are a newly adoptive parent or have been parenting for years, you will find precious gems within the pages of this book. If you are a clinician, using this book as a resource with parents will spark rich conversations and begin shifting paradigms.

PARIS GOODYEAR-BROWN, MSSW, LCSW, RPT-S, founder of Nurture House, director of the TraumaPlay Institute; author of *Trauma and Play Therapy* and *A Safe Circle for Little U*

Mike and Kristin's brilliant work brings easy-to-understand and easily digestible language to the complex issue of childhood trauma and its impact on attachment. An absolute must-read for anyone caring for kids from hard places.

MICHELE SCHNEIDLER, President and COO of 1MILLIONHOME.com

Being able to form and maintain good relationships is critical for healthy development. And it all starts with attachment—the deep early emotional bonds that set the stage for our future relationships. In *Securely Attached*, Mike and Kristin Berry walk the reader through the basics of attachment—how it forms, how it gets disrupted, and what we can do to help heal it. It's a must-read for all adoptive and foster parents.

JOSHUA N. HOOK, PHD, Associate Professor of Psychology at the University of North Texas; coauthor of *Replanted: Faith-Based Support for Adoptive and Foster Families*

Securely Attached is a book that captures the bold but delicate necessity of attachment in a clear and concise way. Parents and caregivers will come away with the opportunity to be open to new understanding about the complexities of attachment, practical ways to take beneficial action, as well as the importance of interactive ways to journal and connect to community along the way. *Securely Attached* is an educational, experiential, and compassionately composed book. A must-read for parents and caregivers who are raising trauma-impacted children.

CARRIE BLASKE, Certified Trainer, Empowered To Connect and Trauma Competent Caregiver

Securely Attached is the book for anyone considering foster parenting or adoption, as well as those on the journey of parenting children with a traumatic history! Mike and Kristin Berry paint a detailed description of the struggles parents will face, and provide practical tools to conquer them. The impact of trauma is real in these children, and in their parents! The more information parents have before fostering or adopting, the better equipped they will be to handle the challenges.

CARRIE O'TOOLE, MA, Adoption and Trauma Life Coach, author of *Relinquished: When Love Means Letting Go*

This is an incredible resource! Finally, a book that focuses on the importance of developing a secure attachment that serves as a guide for caregivers. Developing a secure attachment is the foundation for how we relate to others. You cannot address trauma without addressing how it impacts attachment. Mike and Kristin have filled this book with real-life examples, practical information, and significant encouragement for the journey. This is a must-read book for any caregiver desiring to help their child experience healing and healthy attachments that last a lifetime.

JENN HOOK, MA, founder and executive director of the Replanted Ministry; executive director of the Replanted Conference; coauthor of *Replanted: Faith-Based Support for Adoptive and Foster Families*; therapist and TBRI practitioner

Mike and Kristin Berry have expertly intertwined solid theory and research with life experience in *Securely Attached*. Their approach makes this book informational as well as engaging, a rare result not often found with books based on attachment theory and trauma. I highly recommend *Securely Attached* to parents first being introduced to trauma-informed care, parents in need of a little encouragement, as well as those in the community of foster care and adoption: grandparents, friends, and children's ministry workers.

VALERIE CRANE, executive director of Help One Child, San Francisco, CA

A HANDBOOK FOR ADOPTIVE AND FOSTER PARENTS

Securely Attached

*How Understanding
Childhood Trauma Will
Transform Your Parenting*

MIKE & KRISTIN BERRY

MOODY PUBLISHERS

CHICAGO

Scriptures taken from the Holy Bible, New International Version®, NIV®. Copyright © 1973, 1978, 1984, 2011 by Biblica, Inc.™ Used by permission of Zondervan. All rights reserved worldwide. www.zondervan.com The "NIV" and "New International Version" are trademarks registered in the United States Patent and Trademark Office by Biblica, Inc.™

Edited by Ginger Kolbaba
Interior Design: Kaylee Lockenour
Cover Design: Erik M. Peterson
Cover illustration of hands copyright © 2018 by evtushenko_ira /iStock (1047652524). All rights reserved.
Author photo: Jen Sherrick Photography

The information presented in this book is the result of years of parenting and research by the authors. The information in this book, by necessity, is of a general nature and not a substitute for an evaluation or treatment by a competent medical specialist. The stories in this book are true. The names and circumstances of some of the stories have been changed to protect the anonymity of parents and children.

All websites and phone numbers listed herein are accurate at the time of publication but may change in the future or cease to exist. The listing of website references and resources does not imply publisher endorsement of the site's entire contents. Groups and organizations are listed for informational purposes, and listing does not imply publisher endorsement of their activities.

Library of Congress Cataloging-in-Publication Data
Names: Berry, Mike (Parenting blogger), author. | Berry, Kristin, author.
Title: Securely attached : how understanding childhood trauma will
    transform your parenting, a handbook for adoptive and foster parents /
    Michael and Kristin Berry.
Description: Chicago : Moody Publishers, [2021] | Includes bibliographical
    references. | Summary: "In their twenty-year marriage, Mike and Kristin
    Berry have had the joy of adopting eight children and fostering
    twenty-three. In Securely Attached, they offer practical insights,
    supported by therapeutic and medical facts, so all parents can better
    care for the children in their home who have experienced past trauma"--
    Provided by publisher.
Identifiers: LCCN 2020023277 (print) | LCCN 2020023278 (ebook) | ISBN
    9780802419651 (paperback) | ISBN 9780802498571 (ebook)
Subjects: LCSH: Psychic trauma in children. | Attachment behavior in
    children. | Parent and child. | Foster parents. | Adoptive parents.
Classification: LCC RJ506.P66 B47 2021 (print) | LCC RJ506.P66 (ebook) |
    DDC 618.92/8521--dc23
LC record available at https://lccn.loc.gov/2020023277
LC ebook record available at https://lccn.loc.gov/2020023278

We hope you enjoy this book from Northfield Publishing. Our goal is to provide high-quality, thought-provoking books and products that connect truth to your real needs and challenges. For more information on other books and products that will help you with all your important relationships, go to northfieldpublishing.com or write to:

Northfield Publishing
820 N. LaSalle Boulevard
Chicago, IL 60610

1 3 5 7 9 10 8 6 4 2

Printed in the United States of America

*To our children, who consistently extend grace to us
as we learn to be better parents.*

Contents

A Letter to Our Readers

Dear Friend,

We are so glad you're here. It's been our dream to connect with parents and caregivers like you. As the parents of eight children, all of whom were adopted, we are on this journey with you. Throughout our eighteen years as parents and nine years as foster parents, we have raised all ages and stages. Just like you, we are navigating the rough waters of raising children who have experienced trauma. At times, the all-consuming job of helping our children heal has put a strain on our marriage, friendships, and even our faith. We often felt alone and hopeless. Twenty years ago, when parenthood was only a dream, we thought raising children would come naturally. Instead, our family spent years in crisis. After countless public tantrums, sleepless nights, defiant teens, and distant adult children, we see the value of secure attachments. We learned that we cannot change our children; we can only change ourselves. Through years of research and hands-on experience, we have discovered that secure attachments are at the root of healthy families.

We hope that within these pages you will find a renewed passion for parenting and a perspective shift that moves you toward two important goals:

(1) To create an environment of understanding and safety so your children can form a secure attachment to you;

(2) To create a sense of confidence in yourself and in your parenting so you can build a secure attachment to your children.

Every day as parents we see the toll that trauma experiences have on our children. Helping them heal from trauma and form healthy attachments can feel like an insurmountable task. But the good news is that with a simple shift in thinking, we can change the way we parent, which can lead to healing for our children, ourselves, and our families.

Warmest regards,
Mike and Kristin Berry

CHAPTER 1

EVERYONE EXPERIENCES TRAUMA

Have you experienced trauma? Chances are you have. Take a moment to inventory your trauma exposure. Mark a check next to each personal experience (or tally them mentally). Have you ever:

- Moved to a new home?
- Experienced housing insecurity?
- Experienced a house fire?
- Lived through a natural disaster?
- Changed schools?
- Changed caregivers?
- Experienced a premature birth?
- Had a loved one in the intensive care unit?
- Been verbally abused?
- Felt humiliated publicly?
- Witnessed domestic violence?
- Experienced domestic violence?

- Experienced microaggressions?
- Experienced sexual abuse?
- Broken a bone?
- Stayed in the hospital?
- Been in a war zone?
- Been in a car accident?
- Witnessed someone die?
- Been adopted?
- Been separated from your parents?
- Lived in a foster home?
- Lived with/said goodbye to foster siblings?
- Had a parent leave?
- Lost a loved one to death?
- Witnessed a person struggle with substance abuse?
- Lived with a person with a chronic illness?
- Experienced chronic illness?
- Been divorced?
- Ended a friendship?

Did you check at least one of the items? Of course you did! Chances are, you also felt a physical and emotional response to some of these memories. Though you may not have a physical reaction to your memory of moving to a new home, someone you know may experience a move and immediately be thrown back to when they were homeless as a child. Our life experiences are all tied together and stored in our memory. The seemingly insignificant experiences of one person can open the floodgates of trauma memories for another. At some level, we have all experienced trauma and that trauma experience has changed us.

I (Kristin) grew up in a typical American household. I had plenty of food, clean clothes, and two really nice parents. I am the oldest of four siblings. I went to a good school and lived in a comfortable house. I was never afraid of where my next meal would come from or whether I would have a warm place to sleep. I wasn't exposed to domestic violence, substance abuse, famine, or even natural disaster. When I first heard about the lasting effects trauma can have, I counted myself fortunate never to have experienced trauma. Or so I thought.

In 2012, Mike and I realized the parenting strategies we learned from our upbringings were ineffective. We spent the next eight years sitting at the feet of experts like Dr. Karyn Purvis, Dr. Ira Chasnoff, Julie Alverado, Deborah Gray (LICS), and Sherri Eldridge (adult adoptee and author). We soaked up their knowledge, and our perspective quickly shifted. We learned that trauma exposure changes the way the brain functions and, in cases of severe, chronic trauma, it inhibits the ability to attach in healthy ways. In other words, our children are unable to form a strong emotional bond that typically forms between a child and their caregiver when the child's needs are met. This ability, or inability, to attach and form stable relationships continues with them as they grow older. We began to see our children clearly in the light of this new reality.

A surprising thing happened to us as well. We began to reevaluate our own childhoods. I found that some of my life experiences have shifted my perspective. Throughout my life, I *had* experienced trauma. My mind didn't categorize the trauma as such, but my body and my heart stored the experiences in a way that changed my outlook on the world around me.

You may find it difficult to think in terms of a move being a traumatic experience when we think about soldiers coming home from war or children experiencing years of sexual and physical abuse, so let's clarify exactly what we mean by trauma. Trauma exists in two forms: acute and chronic. Acute is a scary, onetime event; whereas chronic is a distressing event or situation that happens repeatedly or continually over a period of time (we'll talk more about these distinctions in the next chapter). According to Bessel Van Der Kolk, in *The Body Keeps the Score,* "We have learned that trauma is not just an event that took place sometime in the past: it is also the imprint left by that experience on mind, brain, and body."[1]

Trauma can even happen at birth. In *The Primal Wound,* Nancy Newton Verrier describes the trauma that adopted individuals experience: "Many doctors and psychologists now understand that bonding doesn't begin at birth but is a continuum of physiological, psychological, and spiritual events, which begin in utero and continue throughout the postnatal bonding period. When this natural evolution is interrupted by a postnatal separation from the biological mother, the resultant experience of abandonment and loss is indelibly imprinted upon the unconscious minds of these children."[2]

When I thought about our first daughter, whom we adopted at birth, I wondered what trauma she could possibly have. After all, I was at the hospital while she was born. Mike held her in his arms in the nursery and even fed her the first bottle. *Surely she hasn't been traumatized,* I thought. *We've been here the whole time.*

But then it hit me. Our child grew inside of someone else. She listened to that woman's voice and her heartbeat. She felt her emotions and was nourished by her body. Then she lost her. Her mother was gone. The voice, the heartbeat, the familiarity.

Just because our child is a newborn doesn't mean she isn't acutely aware of losing that connection. Acknowledging this loss may be difficult for us, but it is vitally necessary.

Once we got our heads around the concept that everyone has experienced trauma, we began to ask ourselves why our own trauma experiences had not led to catastrophic results in our lives. We wondered where our resiliency came from and became determined to help our children heal, attach, and move forward as we had. But we quickly realized that couldn't happen as long as their past trauma wasn't addressed. So we began researching trauma.

Trauma Changes the Way We See the World and Ourselves

I (Kristin) am fascinated with how things look from different perspectives. I love to take a photo while lying on the floor, camera level to the ground, or while perched atop a chair, camera angled just enough to capture the upturned faces of a room full of birthday celebrators. Both photographs may be of the same room, the same people, even the same day, but the perspective changes the way the viewer feels about the moment. Trauma experiences do the same—they change our perspective. Though we may be in the same room with the same people at the same moment, our experiences have changed the perspective with which we view things around us.

They also change the way we see interactions with others and the way we view our safety and our needs. I love to look at my friends' beautiful social media pages. I was gaining inspiration from a friend's page one night when it struck me that her page looked perfect—all her photographs were flawless, including those with her small children!

"How is this possible?" I asked my teenage daughter. "How do her pictures look so beautiful?"

My daughter glanced at me and shook her head. "It's a filter! No one looks like that!"

She was right. I was viewing my friend's pictures through a filter. The filter made her photos look soft, warm, and lovely. She was doing the same things at her house that I was doing at mine—washing laundry, cooking dinner, and taking her kids to the park—but the filter she placed over those moments changed the way I, the viewer, felt about them. Trauma is like a social-media filter that we carry with us everywhere we go.

Now consider how your children respond to things such as food, loud noises, schedules, strangers, and new experiences—they view them all, even the simplest of things, through the filter of trauma. For instance, a child who has had multiple caregivers may view a day at school as a potential long-term separation from their current caregiver. One of our foster sons packed his toothbrush every day for preschool. One day I (Kristin) crouched next to him as he was getting out of the car and asked, "Why are you taking your toothbrush?" He answered without flinching, "I might never come back to this home and I hate when I have to get a new toothbrush." He smiled a half smile and went inside. I stood dumbfounded. He and I were in the same world, at the same school, at the same moment. My perception of preschool was formed from my own experience of always returning home to the same family. Preschool was fun for me and I never worried about where my toothbrush was during the day.

My foster son's perception of preschool, however, was formed from his experience of losing caregivers without warning. He knew that if he wasn't careful, at a moment's notice, he could lose his toothbrush, along with his caregiver and his home.

That is the effect of trauma. The more Mike and I studied trauma, the better we understood our children's response to common everyday situations—situations that we often take for granted. And when we put understanding trauma into the mix of our parenting, our children's exaggerated reactions to issues like dinner being late, going to the babysitter's house, having plans change, hearing loud noises, or experiencing everyday disappointments make more sense.

The Mind and Body's Reaction to a Memory of Trauma

Last summer on a warm afternoon, I (Mike) took a break from work to head out to our barn to muck the stalls. I love living on a farm, and my barn is my favorite place to be, so keeping it clean gives me a lot of pleasure. With six young children still at home,

I was eager for the time alone. And after several weeks of intense projects within our company, the barn brought a needed change of pace and solitude.

I grabbed a pitchfork and got to work. We have three horses in one stall and that produces a lot of manure! The warm breeze, the horses' gentle neighs, and our chickens' soft clucking relaxed me as I plunged the teeth of the pitchfork into the sawdust and began to sift out the manure. I filled two big scoops into my wheelbarrow. I was lost in my thoughts as I pushed the wheelbarrow out to the mud lot. I caught a glimpse of its contents. It was just manure, but I froze as a memory transported me thirty-five years into the past.

I was an eight-year-old playing at my friend's tobacco farm. As we were playing in the barn, his older sister and her friend tried to force us into a tiny fort we had built for fun. They yelled at us and threatened us. When we didn't move and whimpered out of fear, they laughed. His sister's friend took a stick, walked into the field, and returned with fresh, steaming cow manure. She waved it in our faces and continued to laugh. I was terrified that if I didn't do what she said, she would throw the manure on my clothes, my face, or worse, into my mouth. I wanted to run away as fast as I could, but I couldn't. I was powerless.

Decades later, I tightened my grip on that wheelbarrow of manure as the overwhelming feeling of powerlessness washed over me again. It was as real in my forty-three-year-old body as it was when I was eight. Though the memory didn't ruin the rest of my day, I realized that something that had happened decades ago still caused my body to react.

As caregivers of children with trauma histories, it's crucial that we understand the ways in which a child's trauma history directly impacts behaviors. For instance, consider the child who was not fed properly. They may have a survival response to the need for nutrition. Later, that same child may find security but always have a similar survival response to hunger. It may kick in just because dinner is fifteen minutes late. The parent or caregiver can see that dinner is running behind, but the child is already responding to the situation through the filter of past trauma. Their brain is literally telling them that if they don't eat right now, they might die!

A child can still have a trauma response to everyday situations even after years of having their needs met. They may see that another child has new tennis shoes and immediately their mind tells their body their needs aren't going to be met. The resulting behavior may be to steal that child's shoes (or others just like it), or obsessively ask to wear or borrow the shoes.

Or they may participate in a classroom party where everyone receives a goody bag. As they look around the classroom, they see that someone has a bag that looks bigger than theirs. Their mind views the situation through a trauma filter and tells their body that they are missing out and that they aren't going to get their needs met. The child may drop to the floor and scream, or they may put the contents of the other child's goody bag into their own bag when the child isn't watching. We will talk more about our brains and behaviors as they relate to trauma in upcoming chapters, but for now it's important to understand that when your child behaves in a certain inappropriate way to an event or circumstance, it could be because their mind is seeing it through their trauma filter and telling their body to respond as such.

Understanding Trauma Changes Our Perspective of Our Children and Ourselves

I (Mike) spent the first ten years of our adoption and foster journey concluding that the behaviors I witnessed from some of our children were a "bad child behaving badly." I believed they just needed discipline. Boy, was I wrong. In 2012, Kristin and I attended a conference specializing in helping parents just like us. We gained a simple understanding of trauma, how trauma impacts a child's brain, and how that change impacts the way they see the world around them. In short, this conference was a game-changer for me, and our entire parenting approach. When we educate ourselves, we are able to parent with knowledge, compassion, and understanding, which can lead to helping our children attach better.

During the COVID-19 pandemic, our world has faced a trauma experience collectively. Though we were all faced with the same danger, our reaction to the risk, loss, and uncertainty was as widely varied as the people on this earth. In our own home, we had seven different reactions to each new bit of news. One child, upon finding out that senior prom was cancelled, threw their hands up and declared they were going to drop out of school. Another child, also a senior, cried for two days when she found out that the graduation ceremony had been cancelled. Another child stayed up all night keeping vigilant watch, believing that the virus might turn us into zombies. Another child researched the virus online and washed his hands until they started to bleed. One child ran away, while another sat in their room for days on end, refusing to eat or talk to anyone.

I (Kristin) am sorry to say that I didn't know what to make of their different behaviors. Our children were not thinking or acting rationally. I, too, had spent many sleepless nights worrying about family, friends, lost jobs, and our financial situation. We were all reacting in ways that didn't make sense. My typically go-with-the-flow family was suddenly chaotic. Each day, emotions fluctuated from anger to joy, from sadness to hopefulness, from denial to acceptance. I was ready to lose my mind in the midst of a conversation with one of my older children. Finally, I yelled, "Are you serious? *Everyone* is sad. At least you're alive. Cut this out right now; you aren't making any sense." I stormed out of the house and plopped down on our back porch to collect myself and my emotions.

Just then the phone rang. A good friend, also an adoptive mom, was calling to receive some support of her own. The story she shared with me was eerily similar to mine. She described her son's obsessive behaviors, fly-off-the-handle rage, and preoccupation with conspiracy theories. "I don't know what to do," she told me. "What is happening with him?"

All this loss and uncertainty must be triggering the feelings of aban-donment and loss of control from his childhood, I realized. I nearly smacked myself in the forehead. I could see the trauma reaction so clearly in my friend's son, but I had failed to see it in my own home. From that moment on, Mike and I were able to react differ-ently to our children and empower them to see the virus and the quarantine through new eyes. For our family, though understand-ing trauma didn't relieve us from the feelings of sadness or worry, it did help us identify how our bodies and minds were feeling, and in turn helped us react differently to our circumstances.

In the weeks that followed, all seven of us had a variety of ways to cope with the isolation, fear, and uncertainty. One child made care packages for all her friends and left them on their doorsteps. One child created a movie of her senior year to share with her friends in place of the celebration they were missing. Another child cut hearts out of construction paper to put in our windows to let neighbors know they are not alone. All of them made videos to send to friends, grandparents, and cousins. Some of us spent time alone reading or painting. All of us played cards and board games together. Once we understood our need to process the trauma we were experiencing, along with the trauma memories that all of this was stirring up, we were able to handle the roller coaster of emo-tions with grace.

As parents, it's important to remember that your children's per-ception of things around them are often filtered through the lens of trauma. If your child is responding to a situation in a way that doesn't seem logical to you, ask yourself how the lens of trauma may be changing their perception of what is actually happening. And the important thing to remember is that as you work toward helping them address their trauma and heal from it, you also open new pathways for them to begin securely attaching.

What Now?

- Watch Nadine Burke Harris's TED talk called "How Childhood Trauma Affects Health across a Lifetime." You can find it on YouTube.com.
- Journal or discuss with a friend:
  - How has trauma changed your perspective?
  - Using the list at the beginning of this chapter as a starting point, write about your own trauma experiences. (This stuff is hard, so try using a nice gel pen in a fun color. It may make the task more enjoyable.)
  - How and where can you see that trauma experience as a filter through which you view your community, your family, your personal relationships, and your parenting?
  - What are some ways your trauma experiences have made parenting more difficult?
  - What are some ways your trauma experiences have driven you to become a better parent?
  - Use the list at the beginning of this chapter as a starting point to recognize some of the trauma experiences your child has had. Can you think of others?
  - What are some specific experiences that have affected your child's perspectives? (You may not know everything your child has experienced. That's okay. Learning about and getting to know your child will happen over a lifetime.)

Remember . . .

- *Everyone has experienced trauma.*
- *Every child who was adopted has experienced trauma.*
- *Your child's experiences have changed the lens through which they see the world.*

CHAPTER 2

TRAUMA AND THE BRAIN

What are you doing? Seriously, stop it. Please, just stop it!" Jane found herself shouting at her teenage daughter, Betty, after an hour of trying to calmly reason with her.

Betty had been hoarding food under her bed for months, and when Jane found the foul-smelling stash, Betty began to scream at her. Jane used a gentle tone to explain that the smell was not okay, that the food was rotten, that it was smelling up her room, and that the smell was lingering in the carpet. She brought garbage bags and carpet cleaner into Betty's room and offered to help her clean.

To her increasing frustration, everything she said or did only heightened Betty's response. Instead of accepting her mother's help, Betty insulted her mother, turned on her siblings, threatened to harm herself, and eventually broke down in tears.

Betty's hoarding and subsequent reaction to being discovered made no sense to Jane. They had plenty of food in the refrigerator. The pantry was fully stocked. Betty knew that. She had been living with her family since she was three years old. For thirteen years, Betty had plenty to eat, a safe home, and a loving family.

Jane could see the situation from a logical, rational perspective. Her request for Betty to "just stop it!" is a reaction we often have as parents when our children do something that doesn't make sense. However, it isn't any more reasonable to ask our child to abandon an emotional reaction than it is for us to ask someone in a wheelchair to leave the wheelchair at the door. A person who uses a wheelchair does not cease to need the accommodation just because someone tells them to stop. A person who is having an involuntary reaction to trauma cannot stop just because someone tells them to. That's because trauma has ingrained itself into our children's brains and has shaped the way they interact with the world around them.

Trauma Experiences Leave a Scar

Have you ever broken something and tried to put it back together? I (Kristin) am the oldest of sixteen grandchildren on my mom's side. When my grandfather passed away twenty-one years ago, I was just about to get married. My aunts and uncles sorted through ninety years' worth of memories. Together they gifted me my grandmother's china. The honor was not lost on me. I have gently wrapped and carried each delicate piece to the seven homes I have lived in since, careful not to damage any of it.

A few years ago, two of our children were roughhousing in the kitchen and bumped the shelf where I kept the teacups and saucers. One fell to the ground and shattered. I heard the crash, walked to the kitchen, and knelt to gather the broken pieces.

"I'm sorry, Mommy. I'll glue it," my son said, starting to cry.

I shook my head. "It can't be glued; the damage is too bad."

He tried to fix it, which was sweet, but it was never the same. The break had changed nearly everything about the tiny cup.

Brains are the same way. Trauma experiences are stored inside the brain like tiny shards of broken china. We can mend them, but they cannot go back to exactly the way they were before the experience happened. They are changed.

Simplifying the Brain's Complexity

When we first learned about trauma and its effect on the brain, we found ourselves overwhelmed. Thankfully, we worked with professionals who disentangled the complex information to make it clearer. We found that to appreciate the effects of childhood trauma on our children's brains, we must understand, in a simple way, a few key parts of the brain. We are parents who struggled for years to comprehend our children's behaviors at a surface level. It wasn't until we recognized that trauma changes the brain in a fundamental way that we gained the ability to address behaviors from a perspective of patience, understanding, and healing.

Out of all the brain's complex and unique facets, the three most important for our purposes are the brain stem, the amygdala, and the prefrontal cortex.

The Brain Stem: The Part That Keeps Us Alive

According to William C. Shiel Jr., "The brain stem controls the flow of messages between the brain and the rest of the body, and it also controls basic body functions such as breathing, swallowing, heart rate, blood pressure, consciousness, and whether one is awake or sleepy."[1] The brain stem keeps us alive. It oversees the things we do without thinking, like breathing, heartbeat, pulse, blood flow. The brain stem is also where we retreat when we are alarmed, in danger, or experiencing something intense.

The Amygdala: The Brain's Alarm System

The amygdala filters sensory input to assess potential risk before that information is transferred to the rest of the brain for further processing. The amygdala functions as an alarm system as well as the pleasure sensor, and is thought to play important roles in emotion and behavior.[2] It is best known for its role in processing fear; however, it is also responsible for much of our human behavior. When our amygdala senses the smell of Grandma's apple pie, it processes that input to quickly put our mind at ease. When it senses the smell of smoke, it alerts the brain to potential danger. If danger truly exists, our body becomes prepared to get to safety. If danger doesn't exist—for instance, if the smell of smoke is a campfire—the alarm will quiet and the rest of our brain will process the smell as something anticipated and potentially fun. For people with trauma history, the amygdala plays a crucial role in how they respond to certain high-intensity situations.

The Prefrontal Cortex: Where Logic and Reasoning Live

The prefrontal cortex is located at the front of the brain and is responsible for a person's executive-functioning skills. Executive functioning is responsible for impulse control, planning, decision-making, problem-solving, self-control, and strategizing for long-term goals. Our prefrontal cortex gets us from point "A" to point "B" in the most efficient and successful way possible. Our executive-functioning skills are especially important when it comes to tasks such as getting ready for work or school, following a list of chores or errands, and preparing for the day in time to meet our daily demands. The prefrontal cortex is also where our calm, collected, and reasonable natures live.

So right now, I (Mike) am typing these words while listening to instrumental Christmas music, and I feel calm and peaceful. I am working on this book, following a schedule, and managing my responsibilities as a parent. The prefrontal cortex is responsible for all these behaviors. It's important to note that when we are in an intense situation, the amygdala sounds our brain's alarm, and the prefrontal cortex gets completely overridden.

How Trauma Affects the Brain

When it comes to trauma, how are these three areas of the brain affected? Let's imagine you and I (Mike) are in a lecture hall together. I am standing in front of you talking about, you guessed it, "How trauma changes the brain." In the middle of my discussion, the fire alarm suddenly blares. Then smoke floods through the vents and fills the room. We realize that flames are lapping at the wall behind us. What do we do? We stop what we're doing and move toward the exits. We may become panicked, which causes us to run, push, or claw our way out of the building. What we don't do is stop and discuss what we're eating for lunch. We aren't functioning out of the prefrontal, planning, executive-functioning part of our brain; we are functioning out of our survival brain. You and I would have one goal in mind: *Get out!*

In this situation, here's what's happening in our brains: The amygdala (our alarm system) is telling us, "Danger, danger, danger!" We aren't thinking anymore; our bodies are just reacting. Our brain stem (our survival instincts) takes over. The brain diverts blood and oxygen to the body and away from the prefrontal cortex. This means the prefrontal cortex isn't working. When the amygdala is triggered, it disrupts the place in our brains where logic and reasoning exist. That's why we don't stop in the middle of a smoke-filled room to discuss our favorite movies. We are functioning from our survival brain, which is directing our bodies to safety!

Speaking of feeling safe. Once we make it out of the hot, smoke-filled, potentially fire-ridden building, we stand in the middle of the parking lot feeling frazzled, scared, and panicked. We watch as the fire department roars up and charges into the building. We realize we are safe—that feeling of safety is the prompt that silences the alarm. The amygdala is no longer alerting us, and blood and oxygen are directed back to the prefrontal cortex. We are again able to reason. After thirty minutes or so, we calm down because we are no longer in the path of destruction. By the time the firefighters come out, many of us have resumed our natural states of being. We call this regulation or our baseline of behavior. We'll go deeper into this in later chapters.

What you and I have just experienced would be defined as an acute traumatic situation. Our brains filter daily many less-traumatic reasons for alarm. If I were standing in front of you talking and talking and talking right up to lunchtime, you may begin to feel on edge, because you're getting hungry. Your amygdala warns you that something is wrong, but because this is not a life-or-death situation, your neocortex takes over and processes the information logically. You realize that lunch is in a few minutes, and I'm almost done talking. You may tune me out and think about your favorite foods or you may override your feeling of hunger and force yourself to stay focused.

For a person who has experienced chronic trauma, for instance, in the form of food insecurity, these feelings of hunger may trigger a larger reaction in the moment due to a stored memory of the threat to survival. You may notice your child has a disproportionate reaction to being denied a snack or having to wait five minutes for dinner, which may be because their alarm system has been wired to expect to be hungry. In other words, they go into survival mode.

To explain survival mode, we need to remember the brain stem, which keeps us alive. For instance, it is responsible for breathing. We don't have to think about breathing, it just happens because our brain stem tells our lungs to breathe. When we experience trauma or the memory of trauma, our brain stem can override the rest of our brain, including logic and reason. This is what we often refer to as "survival brain." Our survival brain is like a parking brake. We lived in Cincinnati, Ohio, during the first years of our marriage. Cincinnati is filled with steep hills. Whenever we parked a car in the city, it became a habit to put on the parking brake. If we got into the car and tried to drive without disengaging the break, we found ourselves stuck. The brake had overridden the other systems. Our brains do much the same thing—they have a safety system in place.

Involuntary Actions and the Midbrain

Betty moved in with her foster family at the age of three after living in five different foster homes and multiple stays with biological family members. In her short three years, she experienced food insecurity, housing insecurity, and domestic violence. Betty's new foster family was affectionate and fun loving. They embraced when they felt sad and hugged and high-fived to share joy.

The first time Betty witnessed her foster dad wrestling playfully with her foster brother and sister, she ran to her room in tears and hid under her bed. Her foster parents were shocked and had no idea what had happened. When they remembered her past experience of physical abuse, they understood that their behaviors had triggered a reaction in Betty. They quickly stopped wrestling and crouched next to Betty, assuring her that everything was okay. They smiled softly and told her they were sorry for scaring her.

Betty's foster family eventually adopted her. In the fifteen years that followed that incident, Betty has lived in an environment of safety. She can give and receive hugs and high fives. She voluntarily shows affection to her parents, siblings, and friends. However, she still reacts physically to any touch she doesn't anticipate. She may jump if someone bumps into her on public transportation or shout if her mom pats her on the back unexpectedly. She knows why her body reacts this way but often she is powerless to control her response. She can't just "cut it out." Her brain is filtering the action of touching through her experiences of trauma. Her brain reacts without any logical thought. It's wired that way.

Our brain filters experiences and often reacts in the midbrain without thinking. The midbrain is located at the top of the spinal cord and is responsible for filtering and storing sensory information and motor movement and reactions. That's why we shiver when we're cold or we jump when something surprises us. The midbrain is looking for danger and filters sensory information first before the information makes its way to the neocortex (where the information is processed logically). It has the power to cause us to react without thinking. This is why we jump when we hear a loud noise. Jumping is a reaction—it happens without thought. A split second later, the neocortex gets the information and processes that information using logic. The brain realizes the loud noise is just a door slamming from wind blowing in through an open window. The brain then tells the body to calm down because there is no danger.

Even when we explain rationally to our children why they react in ways they don't need to, they often are unable to do anything about it, because of the reactionary memories that have been placed in their midbrains. This is why a child who has been physically abused may always jump back if someone tries to touch them. Even if the touch is loving, even if the touch is unintentional, even if they know the person doesn't want to hurt them. Trauma experiences change the way our brains react.

Think of Your Child's Brain Like a House

We live in a 1930s farmhouse in central Indiana. Though our first and second floors may be warm and cozy, our basement is creepy. It's an old cellar-style with low ceilings. The floor stays wet most of the year, which leads to a damp musty smell. More than once, the septic tank has backed up and filled our basement with a sludge we won't even dare to describe. Our basement is not a place we spend a lot of time. We have our hot-water heater, furnace, and water softener there. We also have a stack of eight folding chairs in one corner in case we need to escape a tornado. We consider our basement strictly for survival purposes. When we have to go to the basement, we get what we need and we get out.

When it comes to laying a foundation for healthy attachments, the basement represents our survival brain. The main floor, which is warm and welcoming, represents our feeling or emotional brain. In our house, the main floor is where we have the deep (and sometimes difficult) heart-to-heart conversations. It is where we celebrate exciting moments, laugh until our sides hurt, argue, and even shed tears. The second floor, the upstairs, represents our logical brain. Our upstairs has wide-open windows and views for miles. We can see clearly, think, rest, and refresh. It's where our deepest healing takes place.

If we relate our brain to a house, it looks something like this:

Basement: survival only; no learning or relationship building takes place here.

First floor: emotions and feelings live here.

Upstairs floor: logic, learning, resting, and planning take place here.[3]

Basement Brain

A child who has experienced chronic trauma may return to the basement brain often or even become stuck there. We can be tempted as caregivers to try to reason with the child while they are in the basement brain. We simply cannot do this. Survival brain is not the place to create healing, reasoning, or healthy relationships. Our job as caregivers is to enter the basement with the child and help them make their way back upstairs.

We recently had one of our friends ask us how to get her daughter out of her "emotional funk," as she described it. She explained that when her daughter becomes emotional, or does not receive the answer she wants, she cannot be talked to, coerced, or bribed out of this state. We shared how normal parenting tactics to get a child to "snap out of it" rarely work. This is basement-brain dwelling. We have a tendency as parents to expect our children to immediately climb the stairs (so to speak) out of the basement. But they can't. They need assistance. It's our job as caregivers to walk with them and help them climb the stairs to the first-floor brain. (We'll explain how to do this in later chapters.)

First-Floor Brain

The first-floor brain is where we experience our feelings. In our home, we gather around the first-floor's kitchen table, eat warm meals, laugh, relax, and enjoy our time together. We also tend to feel the hard stuff here too. The first floor is where we see sibling rivalry, arguments about curfew, and shed tears over lost friendships. We study for tests, make meals, read books, and pay bills. All these emotions are good; all these activities are part of real life. Emotions are difficult too. They can trigger the brain into thinking it's time to run back to the basement. When our children are in the first-floor brain, a lot of good can happen. However, it's also possible that our children will end up with the alarm sounding that it's all just too much! Often, our children move back and forth from the first floor to the basement brain. They are in a fight for survival, where even the celebratory or "good" moments seem hijacked by the basement brain.

Upstairs Brain

I (Mike) already feel myself longing for that coveted Sunday afternoon nap in our loft, as the warm sun floods through the window and creates a toasty atmosphere. This is the upstairs. It's the epicenter of peace and comfort. This is removed from the survival mode of the basement and even the emotional environment of the first floor. When we're talking about our children's emotions and behaviors, the upstairs-floor brain is the peaceful, logical brain. This is where we must lead our children.

Not All Trauma Is the Same

All trauma experiences change the way our brain filters and responds to the world around us. But not all trauma experiences are the same. As we mentioned briefly in chapter 1, there are two primary types of trauma: acute trauma and chronic trauma—and both shape the brain.

Acute Trauma

Acute trauma can be described as a scary or intense onetime event. This onetime event could have a profound impact on the way we react to certain reminders of the event. My (Kristin's) brother was in a car accident last year. He and his family were injured, and healing has been a long and often grueling process. Even though the accident happened only once, their bodies and minds remember the event each time they drive past the site or the hospital, hear emergency-vehicle sirens, or visit the places in the community they had been just prior to the accident.

Acute trauma can linger in a person's mind and change the way they live long after the event took place. That is because the trauma experience is stored in the brain. Picture the person who lives a fairly normal life, but suffered the sudden loss of a child years earlier. The child's bedroom is closed up tight with everything still in its place, frozen in time. The parent cannot talk about their child without tearing up, and every holiday is marked with deep depression. The person who suffers a horrific car accident may be afraid to make left turns. The person who was robbed at gunpoint in their younger years hates to be alone or feels paralyzed if outside after dark. Though acute trauma may not affect our every moment, it does leave a lasting memory.

Some examples of acute trauma:

- Experiencing a home fire
- Losing a job
- Being the new kid at school
- Moving from one house to another
- Losing a friend
- Losing a loved one to death
- Being in a car accident
- Witnessing something intense or horrific
- Being a victim of sexual or physical assault that happened once
- Having major surgery
- Being in financial duress
- Living through a natural disaster

Most of us experience acute traumatic situations. Earlier this year, I (Mike) was on a flight home and had a connection at Chicago's Midway International Airport. As I flew toward Midway, I looked out my window and spotted an enormous, old, dilapidated building. It took up two city blocks. Suddenly my body filled with anxiety. Odd, right? But this was no coincidence. We were flying over Gary, Indiana, and that building was the ruins of City Methodist Church. In the summer of 2013, I visited that church with a film crew from the church I was working with at the time. We were there to film a documentary-style video in the building. As the team and I were scouting the location, we witnessed men smash in the windshield of one of our vehicles. It sent the entire team into panic. In "fight-or-flight" intense situations, I am a "flight" response, so I immediately began looking for ways to get out of there.

It took us a solid eight hours for our bodies to calm down. The next day was fairly normal for all of us. No one remained traumatized from the event. Our logical brains processed the onetime event and categorized it as such. However, nearly six years later, at an altitude of eight-thousand feet, safely above City Methodist Church, the anxiety from that fateful summer day returned to me like a flood. That's the impact acute trauma can have on a person. My entire life wasn't changed, but my brain held on to the trauma and affected my body's response.

Chronic Trauma

Chronic trauma is a distressing experience that happens repeatedly or continually over a period of time. Foster and adoptive children have often experienced repeated traumatic situations that have lasted over their lifetimes. Remember Betty who lived with five foster families and multiple family members before the age of three? Through that experience, she learned that caregivers cannot be counted on. Even after more than a decade of having Jane as her mother, Betty's brain still filters their relationship through her experiences of loss. Though she doesn't purposely do that, the trauma shaped her brain to respond that way.

Some examples of chronic trauma:

- Prolonged abuse
- Neglect
- Malnourishment
- Food insecurity
- Housing insecurity
- Multiple caregivers over a short period of time
- Witness to domestic violence
- Living in a highly volatile environment
- Living in a dangerous environment
- Living in a war zone or experiencing war
- Terminal illness

Let's consider how chronic trauma affects our children who were in a repeatedly volatile situation, continually hungry, abused, or threatened. The same thing that happens in an acute traumatic situation happens in a chronic traumatic situation. The amygdala sounds the alarm, the prefrontal cortex is overridden, and the child moves into their brain stem (survival mode). The difference, however, is that the trauma continues and the amygdala does not calm down. The prefrontal cortex stays overridden, and the child resorts to living in a state of survival.

Imagine experiencing a car crash every single day. You don't know when it's going to happen but it is guaranteed to happen every day. How would you feel? How would you interact with the world around you? Would you be free to emotionally connect or attach to other people? Your body and your mind would be tense all the time just waiting for the trauma to happen. People who experience chronic trauma live in this constant state of survival—and that affects their ability to securely attach with you and others in your family. The good news is that even though trauma shapes the brain, healing and healthy emotional connections can happen.

What Now?

- To learn more about the brain, watch National Geographic's "The Human Brain, Explained": https://www.nationalgeographic.com/science/health-and-human-body/human-body/brain/.

- To learn an easy way to remember the three parts of the brain, go to our website: https://www.thriveparents.org/understandingtrauma/.

- Journal or discuss with a friend:
  - Write or talk about a time when you reacted to something without thinking (a loud noise, an off-hand comment, an emotional television show, or a distinct smell). Were you confused by your reaction? How did your body feel when it reacted that way? Did you realize right away why you reacted that way or did it take you a while to process the sensory input logically?

- Watch Paris Goodyear-Brown's TedxTalk on trauma and play therapy: https://www.youtube.com/watch?v=SbeS5iezIDA

Remember . . .

- *Trauma changes the way our brain processes information.*
- *The brain can respond involuntarily to sensory input.*
- *Sometimes the brain's response to an experience doesn't seem to make sense.*

CHAPTER 3

RESILIENCY AND HEALING

Charlie and Calvin went to live with Patty and Frankie when Charlie was two years old and Calvin was eleven months. They'd been living with their second foster family at the time parental rights for them were terminated. A couple of years later, when the boys became legally available for adoption, Patty and Frankie welcomed them. As foster parents, they knew the children would need time for adjustment, yet they found themselves frustrated and concerned as caring for Charlie and Calvin took extra effort to help them feel safe and to build trust.

Charlie could not be consoled when he was upset. At the slightest change in the schedule, or brief interaction with a stranger, he launched into screaming tirades that lasted for hours. Patty often had to hold Charlie (who was growing heavier by the day) for hours on end. Calvin was also inconsolable, but instead of screaming, he became harmful to others and often destructive to personal property. Both Patty and Frankie often found themselves chasing after him, trying to comfort him while protecting their belongings and their loved ones. They discovered that even children at such young ages who have experienced trauma are not as naturally resilient and that they do not "just bounce back."

Children who experience chronic trauma don't have healthy resilience abilities, which makes it difficult for them to attach securely. But as their caregivers, we can help them build resiliency and heal so they *can* attach securely.

What Is Resiliency?

We often hear "Children are resilient!" It's true that children seem to bounce back quickly from all types of undesirable situations. I (Kristin) watched our two-year-old son race through the house with one leg in a full cast just a week after tumbling down our stairs. He was not hindered in the least by his previous injury. Our other son, barely recovered from the stomach flu, was caught leaping from one couch to the other, laughing gleefully.

One child may be curled up on the couch reading a good book while his mother and father scream at each other just one room away. Another child may smile joyfully at every new foster family and shake off any question of comfort, insisting she is fine and that moving doesn't phase her anymore. Each of these situations is an indicator of the child's ability to cope, adapt, and survive. It is not, however, an indicator of the child's actual emotional well-being.

To the question "How resilient are children?" Darcia F. Narvaez, professor of psychology at the University of Notre Dame, answers: "If you look at the whole picture of health and well-being, not that much." She points to the ACE (Adverse Childhood Experiences) study, "which estimates that 2/3 of American adults had adverse experiences as children that are negatively affecting their health and well-being. The effects of abuse, neglect and trauma on physical and mental health are longterm, even with interventions. . . . To thrive, children's needs must be met. In early life that means constant touch, no distress . . . multiple responsive adult caregivers, free play in nature, not to mention laughing and joyful social relations."[1]

Since a lot of this was missing with our children in their early lives, we must do everything in our power to repair these crucial disrupted moments of attachment. To think that a child is resilient enough to move through trauma experiences without support is a misunderstanding that can carry lifelong consequences.

While it is true that children can be resilient, it is also true that we can build resiliency over time. What exactly is resiliency? According to Dr. Michael Unger, family therapist and professor of social work at Dalhousie University, "In the context of exposure to significant adversity, resilience is both the capacity of individuals to navigate their way to the psychological, social, cultural, and physical resources that sustain their well-being, and their capacity individually and collectively to negotiate for these resources to be provided in culturally meaningful ways."[2] To put it simply, resiliency is the ability to bounce back after an undesirable experience.

This is how it works. The brain stores memories of all experiences. Though we may not remember each experience specifically, our brains have gathered data from every encounter. The brain saves that data, which becomes the filter through which it weighs new experiences. If a child experiences discomfort but the discomfort is quickly remedied, the child's brain stores the experience and expects for future discomfort to come to an end. A child learns that when they need help, help will come. As the child matures, the child learns to remedy their own discomforts as they happen. Each time the discomfort happens, the child's brain bounces back. If and when the child experiences trauma, their brain already knows how to bounce back. Though it will take longer to recover from a car accident than a poopy diaper, for instance, recovery will happen.

We build resiliency through a number of different factors:

Healthy Body and Mind

I (Mike) like to think about our brain and body as the general and first officer of our functionality. The brain gives the orders, and the body carries them out. Think about your typical day. You have errands to run, tasks to accomplish, projects to complete—the list goes on and on. The way you continue day after day to be productive is through your own resiliency. The way you achieve resiliency is through rest—the rest and renewal that come with getting enough sleep, eating healthy food, and participating in positive relationships. As I write this, it's early in the morning, and I just had a good night's rest. The words flow from my brain, through my fingers, and onto this screen. Last night, when I was exhausted, I couldn't write one thing.

The same is true for our children. They need proper rest, healthy food, and loving relationships. When our children have these key ingredients, their bodies can replenish for a new day of activity, learning, and personal growth.

Connection to Community

For the past fifteen years, we have become intentional about connecting with families just like ours. In the summer of 2017, we traveled to a summer family camp with foster and adoptive families. One of the comments we heard from a few of our kids throughout the week was, "The kids I've met are just like me, and they have a family just like ours. I didn't have to explain how our family was built. They got it!"

This simple connection helped our children know two things: First, they were not alone. Other children had experienced the same past trauma as they had, and were now growing up in the same kind of family as they were. Second, and probably the most important, while life may have hard moments and seasons, in the long run, it was going to be okay.

Often as a family of faith, our children have been encouraged to deny the hard parts of their story and focus on all the "good that God has done." While God *has* done good, He also meets us exactly where we are. Our God grieves with us, comforts us in our loss, and rejoices with us in our joy. When our children met other families of faith who were feeling the same range of emotions as they were, it was as if a mental door opened. They could love God and still feel sad. They could love their family and still miss their first family. They could feel angry about their adoption and grateful for their adoption all in the same breath. Being in community with other foster and adoptive families is a vital aspect of resiliency.

Healthy Family Relationships

We have several nonnegotiable values as a family. We eat dinner together almost every night, we read Scripture together and pray every Sunday at lunchtime, at least once a week we do an activity together, we travel with just family on vacation, we look out for one another, and we believe families always stick together. There's rarely a week that goes by when our children don't hear one of us repeat one of these values to them. Why? Because family relationships are important. We want our children to know that wherever they go in life or in the world, their family connection remains. This is how we recover through life's biggest storms. This is how we stay healthy and true to ourselves.

Healthy family relationships are crucial in the resilience process because these are the people who continue to believe in us, love us, and support us, regardless of the ups and downs. Right now, as our two senior daughters face an unforeseen circumstance with the rest of their senior year being cancelled as a result of the COVID-19 pandemic, they are able to stay emotionally strong because we as a family are surrounding them and grieving with them through this.

Safety

A sense of safety and security is a major contributing factor to resiliency. Several years ago we were in a training seminar for foster parents where the instructor used the phrase *felt safety*. The instructor shared how felt safety is something all of our children need, but it isn't something they immediately experience upon entering our homes. She asked one of the couples: "Is your home safe?" The couple said yes. "What about heating and cooling? Is it warm in the winter and cool in the summer?" Again, yes. "Do you have enough food in your pantry, clean water coming out of your faucets?" Yes to all of that. Then she asked something that struck a major chord for all of us: "Do the children entering into your home know all of this to be true?"

We know our homes are safe. We know *we* are safe. But do our children know? When a child feels safe, they are more likely to think clearly and function productively. When they don't feel safe, their mind is clouded, their judgment impaired, and they function from their survival brain.

Access to Resources

A few years ago, our family attended a church in Indianapolis. I (Kristin) was employed there, working primarily by helping people connect to the resources that would aid in rehabilitation. I spent most of my time working with people who had housing insecurities, food insecurities, had lost their children to the welfare system, were dealing with landlords who were taking advantage of them, or were trying to get back on their feet after a prison sentence. One of the most heartbreaking things I witnessed were families who had lost everything and lacked the resources to care for their children. Yet with access to food, housing, steady income, and relationships within the community, these families thrived.

As I consider their situations, I watch as my children come down from their bedrooms after a long night's rest, open cabinets, and pull out cereal, bagels, or bread. As simple as it sounds, there is a deep security in knowing they have access to resources such as food when they need it. In our own home, we still see the effects of past trauma, but consistent access to resources builds confidence in our children as they heal.

Identification with a Culture, People Group, or Religion

We have a multiracial family. Until five years ago, we lived and worked in a nearly all-white community in the suburbs of Indianapolis. We thought we were putting our children in the best school with the most resources. We thought our community was diverse enough. We thought our kids would fit in and that they would have everything they needed. We were wrong; our children did not fit in. They felt lost and without an identity. And we felt terrible.

We soon recognized the importance of connecting our children to a more diverse culture. As a result, we found a school that was a perfect fit for our daughters, so beginning in the ninth grade, we transferred them to the new school. The environment was racially and economically diverse and focused on the arts.

Diversity is important to us for all of our children, but most importantly for our children of color. More than that, it's a high value for us to connect our children to a diverse culture where they can interact with students like them as well as those who are vastly different. We wish we would have made this change when they were babies. Though we can't go back, we can be intentional moving forward. It is our job as parents to help our children connect to friends, mentors, teachers, and coaches who have similar life experiences to them. As they grow up, they will need to be able to connect to a community of their own.

Healthy Environment at Home and in the Community

Ask yourself if your church, neighborhood, youth sports organizations, or social circles are healthy for your children. In addition, does your home environment promote resiliency and healthy attachments? One of the reasons we decided to end our foster care license in 2012 was this very question. We recognized that the revolving door of foster placements and caseworkers was causing insecurity for our children who were living with us permanently. We have had to examine our house of worship, neighborhood, friendships, schools, and interaction with family members. We have had to make difficult changes in order to create an environment of safety for our children in our home and in the community. Being willing to change for the benefit of our children has opened doors to friendships, relationships, and experiences we never would have had as a family if we had been too afraid to change.

Caregivers Who Can Meet Needs

Children recover from trauma histories, heal quicker, and thrive in environments where they are safe and well cared for and where their needs are met. Some of our close friends adopted a son who had gone through horrific abuse before going into their care. When the child first entered their home, his behaviors were impulsive, erratic, and even unsafe at times. But because our friends were equipped to meet his needs and help him through the healing process, after just a few years, they began to see drastic improvements. Today, five years later, their son is not the same child who entered their home at a very young age. They still have a long road to go with him, but he is recovering day by day because he's in an environment where he's well cared for.

Our greatest ability to bounce back from trauma is directly related to our attachments, specifically the bond between a caregiver and a child, which sets the foundation for all other relationships in a person's lifetime. A child who has healthy attachments has learned to navigate the world around them. They can more quickly bounce back after experiencing a trauma.

Resiliency is like a rubber band: a child with healthy attachments can be stretched by a traumatic experience and then rebound. A child who is stretched to the limit over and over will be like an overstretched rubber band—they won't bounce back so easily. Gracie is the teenage daughter of a family friend. When she was a preteen she came into their home through foster care. During this time she still had visits with her first mom. Her mom was inconsistent with her visits. For the first several months, Gracie made excuses for her. Toward the end of the eighth month in foster care, Gracie stopped making excuses for her mother. She became angry and resentful, and often she took these emotions out on her foster parents and herself. Her foster parents stood beside her no matter what. Over the next five years, Gracie began to trust her foster parents. She was able to process her past trauma and her damaged relationship with her mother. She worked with a therapist and her foster parents to learn healthy ways to cope with her feelings. Because of her growing attachment to her parents, she was able to have a solid place to land when she was feeling insecure.

Primarily, resiliency is built through relationships with caregivers. An infant will feel distress at feeding time or when their diaper needs to be changed. The caregiver will meet this need almost immediately. In this way, the infant learns to bounce back from the uncomfortable situation. As the child grows, they will encounter many stressful situations, but as those situations occur, the child's caregiver continues to meet each need. Over time the child will gradually gain independence. The preschooler will take initiative in making simple snacks and using the toilet by herself. The grade schooler will ask a teacher for help with a difficult math problem. The preteen will talk with a mentor about a tough situation they experienced at school. A high schooler will seek counsel from a friend before making a big decision. An adult will lean on loved ones during times of trouble. At each age and stage, they have learned to trust that stressful situations won't last forever; they have discovered how to use healthy and appropriate resources to meet their own needs. They have learned to do this by interacting with trusted caregivers who met their needs first. This is healthy resiliency.

Resiliency in a Onetime Traumatic Event

When I (Kristin) was ten years old, I was riding my bike with my sister. We were racing down the sidewalk when I hit a bump, flipped over my handlebars, and landed directly on my face. I was scraped and bruised all over and I was spitting out pieces of teeth. While my sister went to get my parents, our neighbor scooped me up and took me home. My mom stayed by my side while I inspected the damage I'd done to my face and my beautiful new adult teeth. I was devastated, but she kept her cool and drove me to the emergency dentist who fixed my teeth as best he could. Though I'm still self-conscious of my chipped front teeth, the event doesn't have much impact on my everyday life. Within a week of the accident, I went back to riding my bike and learned to be more cautious. Because of my healthy attachment to my caregiver, what could have been a life-altering experience became barely a blip on the radar of my childhood.

My nephews, who experienced the car accident with their parents a few years ago, which we talked about in chapter 2, have bounced back as well, even though their experience was much more traumatic than simply losing teeth. They experienced the crash itself, they witnessed their mother (my sister-in-law) injured, they watched as the jaws of life cut through their car doors to free them, and they were taken to separate hospitals away from their parents.

They were bruised and shocked, but they were safe enough to return home that night. Their aunts and uncles picked them up at the hospital and took them home.

My sister and I stayed with them while their mom recovered in the hospital and their dad attended to her. My sister and I did our best to make them feel comfortable and normal, but the kids weren't used to us, they had never stayed alone with us before, and they were uncertain of what to make of us. It took months for their mother to recover, and through that time they had to adjust to a new sense of normal. They had trouble sleeping, worried about the hospital, ambulances, and their parents. However, they didn't stay in that initial state of shock. Today they are happy, healthy, and whole as a family. My sister-in-law is the picture of perseverance, my brother is a model of strength, and my nephews are the poster children for resiliency. Why?

My nephews bounced back because they had a solid foundation to bounce back to. They had their needs met even before they were born. They have grown up in an environment where their caregivers are consistent, trustworthy, responsible, loving, and predictable. When a traumatic experience rocked their world, they were changed by the experience but they found their way back to peace because that way had been paved by those who cared for them. This is good news for you, if you are caring for children who have experienced something scary or intense. Your consistency and ability to provide a stable environment will help your children recover and heal.

Resiliency When a Child Experiences Chronic Trauma

Years ago, I (Kristin) was working in an after-school program. One child in particular always had difficulty sitting still. Every time a male volunteer entered the room, his elbows would fly up from his side and he would jump to his feet. Most of the other volunteers took this to be an act of disobedience. We knew it was much more. His behavior was the product of an abusive stepfather. He had experienced this to such a degree that his brain was conditioned to expect that every time an adult male entered the room, the child was going to be beaten.

When the brain's alarm system sounds continuously because of chronic trauma, which overrides the prefrontal cortex and the systems of rational thinking, the brain develops a "glitch." It now expects to experience trauma and is conditioned to function from the brain stem. The amygdala may perceive a situation of danger where no danger exists or the amygdala may be desensitized to the danger that is actually present. The brain may panic, throwing the person into a survival response. Their ability to bounce back has been stretched to the limit and has lost its elasticity. The person who experiences chronic trauma will have a harder time with resiliency than a person who has experienced acute trauma.

This is why resiliency in children with chronic trauma is not as simple as "They'll get over it," "They're young enough that they won't remember a thing," "This isn't trauma, it's manipulation," or "All kids are resilient; they'll bounce back." In order for these kids to attach securely to us and eventually to others, we have to intentionally help them build resiliency.

Helping Your Child Build Resiliency after Trauma

When I (Mike) was six years old and my sister was four, our parents took us to Portland, Oregon, for a family wedding. While we were there, our parents met up with friends in the lobby restaurant of the hotel. They employed two teenage caregivers over us while they were away. For the next three hours, the boys tormented my sister and me. They even locked me out of the hotel room. I could hear my sister cry and call for me through the hotel room door. When they finally opened the door, they bolted past me down the hallway and around a corner, disappearing before I could catch up to them. As my appointed caregivers, I recognized that I needed to stay with them. Plus, my mom told me I needed to. They laughed, but as my sister and I chased them, we became frantic. Every door and light fixture looked the same, carpet patterns blended, and I had no idea what room number was ours. Eventually my sister and I made our way to the hotel lobby and located our parents.

Though I was proud of myself for finding my parents, for years afterward, I felt afraid whenever my parents left me for any reason. However, my parents remained consistent. They always returned home, and I was never truly alone. I began to trust that my parents would provide safety for me even in their absence. And I was able to trust my parents to help me. I knew how to find them and I was able to get to safety. I was able to do this because my mom and dad laid the foundation of trust and attachment for me.

For you as a caregiver through foster care or adoption, by providing a consistent and stable environment for your children, where you are building security and trust, you can help them build resiliency. In *The Body Keeps the Score,* Bessel Van Der Kolk asks, "Is it possible to help the minds and brains of brutalized children to redraw their inner maps and incorporate a sense of trust and confidence in the future?" He concludes:

> Traumatized human beings recover in the context of relationships: with families, loved ones, AA meetings, veterans' organizations, religious communities, or professional therapists. The role of those relationships is to provide physical and emotional safety, including safety from feeling shamed, admonished, or judged, and to bolster the courage to tolerate, face, and process the reality of what has happened.[3]

Resiliency is what helps us accept care from others as well as find resources to meet our own needs. We help our children move forward by remaining a consistent, loving presence in their lives. Because of what they went through in their past, they may believe we may suddenly leave them. We reinforce resiliency by sticking it out with them, even when it becomes messy. Resiliency drives us to connect in relationships, seek counseling, visit the doctor, use coping skills, and accept help. Resiliency shows us how strong we really are. It is in that recognition of our own inner strength and the strength of our communities that we find healing.

What Now?

- For more information and resources on resiliency, check out centerforresilientchildren.org.
- Journal or discuss with a friend:
  - Tell about a time when you bounced back from a difficult situation.
  - How did you feel when you were experiencing a stressful situation?
  - Whom did you lean on?
  - How did your support system help you?
  - What parts of your personality aided in your resiliency?
  - What three practical things can you do to support your child in building resiliency?
  - In what one way can you intentionally meet your child's needs today?
  - What is one way you can validate your child's emotions and needs?

Remember . . .

- *Resiliency is strengthened through trusting relationships.*

- *Repeated trauma is like an overstretched rubber band; it can cause a person to lose the ability to bounce back.*

- *Even though a child has experienced chronic trauma and has been overstretched, they are able to heal.*

CHAPTER 4

ATTACHMENT AND HEALING

Before I (Kristin) was born, my mother took care of me. She went to the doctor, ate healthy food, and waited with anticipation for my arrival. When I was born, I imagine the doctor delivered me and placed me on my mother's chest. She looked at me with love and an overwhelming desire to care for me. (I am also quite certain she thought I was the most beautiful baby on the planet, though this theory has been neither confirmed nor denied.) My mother cradled me and, in time, she handed me to my father. They fed and diapered me. They took me home and placed me in a cradle in front of their cozy wood-burning stove, and before long, family came to meet me. My grandmother stayed with us and aided in my care. Loving people surrounded me and made sure my every need was met.

As I grew older, I attended preschool with Mrs. Greene, who was amazing. I can still hear her voice in my memory. She was sweet and creative and fun. While I was at preschool, she made sure I received my healthy snacks, washed my hands after using the potty, and was delivered to the correct parents at the end of each day.

Later, I attended elementary school and met teachers and friends I had never known before. I enjoyed relationships outside of my family, but my parents were always there at the end of the day to take me home. As a teen I enjoyed going to summer camp, playing sports, and starting my first part-time job. My friendships deepened and I even had romantic interests. Through college and into young adulthood, I wasn't yet relationally independent, so I asked my parents' advice on everything from money to boyfriends to simple car maintenance.

Eventually I formed new lifelong attachments to my husband and my children. I have friends who are like brothers and sisters. These additions have not taken away from my first attachments. They are an outpouring of relational abilities I formed with my very first caregivers.

Even today, I appreciate and respect my parents' opinions, advice, and support. I weigh friendships, job opportunities, and relationships with my own family on the scale of attachments that my parents first built with me.

For me, secure attachments formed naturally, over time. I was able to enjoy secure attachments because the healthy and loving bond my caregivers gave me as a child set the foundation for all other relationships thereafter. We form secure attachments when our needs are met, consistently, over time. Secure attachments lead to independence and the ability to form healthy relationships throughout a lifetime. But what about those children who do not form healthy attachments early on? How can we help them form those attachments?

First let's consider more in-depth what attachments are and why they are so important.

The Benefits of Healthy Attachments

When we experience healthy attachments, we receive benefits that last throughout our lives and help us navigate relationships, challenges, and other issues in a stronger way. As we discussed in the previous chapter, we know that resiliency is a powerful benefit of healthy attachments. But it isn't the only benefit. Let's look at six others that come about because of healthy attachments.

1. They Lay the Groundwork for Connection to Family and Friends

Over the past twenty years, we have built close friendships with two couples who are also foster and adoptive families. We all met long ago, before any of us had children, while working in a church youth ministry. Together we have weathered the storms of job loss, grief, and terminal illness. We have also celebrated births, birthdays, adoption days, new jobs, weddings, and the arrival of grandchildren. We vacation together as couples and families and we are always up for a last-minute cookout at one of our houses.

Friendships aren't always easy; they take work just as all relationships do. Throughout the years, we all have persevered with patience, communication, and time. There is no doubt we are stronger because of our friendships. But where did we learn to be connected in this way? We learned from our healthy attachments as children.

I (Kristin) learned to show up for people when they need support because my parents show up for me. Mike learned to be a good host because he watched his parents invite friends and family into their home. Our early experiences with attachment create a map for us to follow throughout our lifetimes.

2. They Give Us the Ability to See Ourselves through Others' Eyes

When I (Kristin) was a little girl, I looked forward to visits with my grandmother. To her, my blonde hair was "golden silk." My freckled face was "kisses from the sun." She saw me quite differently from how I saw myself. I was awkward, skinny, and covered in freckles. I never felt good enough, and those insecurities overshadowed everything I did. As I grew older, her opinion of me stayed with me. When kids in junior high teased me or a boy didn't think I was pretty, or a friend didn't like me, or an employer treated me with disrespect, part of what got me through those difficult times was that I remembered the feeling of being valued, which my grandmother instilled in me through our healthy attachment.

3. They Teach a Child How to Function within the Community

MaryJane is securely attached to her family. She knows they will support her no matter what. Through their support, she also learned to give support. As a child, she helped with dishes and laundry. When she got older, she practiced taking just the amount of cereal she was going to eat for breakfast. She understood she was part of something bigger than herself and knew that using more than her fair share would potentially take away from another family member. When MaryJane was a young adult, her attachment to her family translated to attachment to community. When her town was hit by a tornado, she was on the front lines of cleanup. She even volunteered to collect food and clothing for the families affected. MaryJane's attachment to family formed the foundation for her to attach to her community.

4. They Anchor Us to Our Family and Community

When we have healthy attachments that anchor us, we have freedom to venture out into the world. When I (Kristin) was a child, my family owned a boat. Every summer, we took it out on a lake for long days of swimming, fishing, and exploring. We could take the boat to an island where we hiked all day, or we could anchor far from shore and dive off the deck into the cool, fresh water. We never worried about venturing from the boat because we knew it was securely tethered to one location. A secure attachment is like an anchor to our family and community—it gives us the freedom to leave and know the people we love will be there when we get back.

5. They Ground Us

Healthy attachments remind us of where we come from and what is real. Katy was adopted by Rob and Anne Marie when she was three years old. She'd experienced significant childhood trauma, so she isn't sure about her attachment to her family. Sometimes she drifts from them or makes impulsive choices that often lead to danger. She has a hard time knowing who to trust or what actions are safe. Because her family knows the value of healthy attachment, they continually pursue her. Slowly, as Katy has grown into adulthood, Rob and Anne Marie are seeing healing, as Katy is recognizing who they are and the love they have for her. Even though building this attachment has taken years of consistency on Rob and Anne Marie's part, Katy is starting to more securely attach and navigate the world around her with a clearer head.

6. They Can Protect Us from Danger

In addition to my (Mike's) parents caring for me and meeting my greatest needs, they also taught me, through our relationship, what was safe, unsafe, trustworthy, and what to be cautious of. That's because they provided healthy attachments. In *The Body Keeps the Score*, Bessel Van Der Kolk writes that "our attachment bonds are our greatest protection against threat."[1] According to Van Der Kolk, we have a greater line of defense around us when we are securely attached to people who care about us or have our best interest in mind. This keeps us from making decisions that can endanger our lives—such as running away and being trafficked.

How Healthy Attachments Lay the Foundation for All Relationships

Our attachments to one another drive nearly everything we do. We are born to be in relationship with others. It is because of that drive that we maintain relationships with the family we were born into as well as one day form families of our own. It is because of our need for connection that we care well for our children, not only physically but emotionally.

We know who to trust based on our past experiences. We understand the give-and-take of relationships based on the attachment we build first with caregivers. We know how to be a trustworthy person because of the trust formed in childhood experiences. We know how to recover from stress, discomfort, and trauma because we first learn from our caregivers.

As you consider your own childhood, you may have a snapshot of what a healthy or secure attachment looks like. But how does this look developmentally through early childhood, adolescence, and into adulthood? Let's look at a few examples.

The Content Baby

A baby who knows her needs will be met may sleep well, eat heartily, and relax in her mother's arms. This baby cries when her diaper is dirty, when she is hungry, lonely, in pain, or afraid. She doesn't cry for long, though, because her mother and father meet her needs as quickly as possible. She learns that she can trust her caregivers. She begins to self-soothe as she grows older. She finds her own pacifier and pops it back into her mouth.

The Curious Toddler

Have you ever noticed that toddlers don't usually take their first steps toward their parents? They typically take their first steps toward some type of fantastic adventure, like an uncovered electrical outlet or the corner of a coffee table. They are curious about everything. They explore all the dangers their tiny world has to offer but they do so with their caregivers firmly in their sights. Toddlers may refuse to go to Grandma or the babysitter. They may prefer Mom or Dad to all others.

The Secure Preschooler

A three- to five-year-old who feels secure in his relationships with his caregivers begins to explore the world outside of home. He may attend a preschool, form friendships in the community, or begin little-tykes sports. He often feels nervous when leaving caregivers and may cry for a while when being dropped off someplace away from home. However, he is quickly reassured that caregivers will return. And his trust is strengthened because they do return.

The Elementary Explorer

A child between ages five and twelve may still like to be tucked into bed at night and he may want Mom or Dad to listen intently to his made-up plays or his latest obsession with a new video game. He is discovering his own likes and dislikes. His identity is less attached to his parents' identity as he is exploring new friendships, relationships with teachers, and the dynamics of after-school clubs and sports. He ventures out into the world but quickly returns home to the structure of his own environment and the security of his caregivers.

The Boundary-Pushing Teen

The teenager may challenge curfew, family values, and responsibilities. This same teenager may curl up on the couch next to you or call you on a break from work just to talk. She is listening to everything you say, even though it looks like she isn't listening at all. She may try new friendships and new activities as she explores the wide world around her.

The Emotionally Grounded Young Adult

The young adult has his own voice. He chooses whom to date, where or if to go to college, what type of job he will hold, and what lifestyle he will lead. He comes home for Christmas or maybe every weekend. He may live out of town only calling once a week or he may live a few streets over in the hopes that he can pop by for some of Mom and Dad's home cooking. He is becoming secure in who he is as a person but still calls his parents for advice or support.

The Married (Adult) Child

She feels confident in her role as an adult. She starts her own home, and she and her spouse model it after their homes growing up. She and her spouse compromise as they choose which parts of their childhood homes they will imitate and which they will change. They value the thoughts and ideas of their own families but are secure in who they are as individuals. They make their own healthy choices about their home, finances, meals, friendships, and careers.

The Child Becomes the Parent

The child who is now a parent still seeks his parents' advice and wisdom when needed. He also knows how to find answers for himself and for their child. He and his spouse will choose their own pediatrician, schools, childcare, diet, church, and community. They will model some of their parenting after their own parents, while other things they choose will be drastically different.

These are all healthy attachments. But what do disrupted attachments look like?

When a Person Forms an Unhealthy Attachment

In our backyard we have a beautiful evergreen tree. Last summer we noticed another tree growing up alongside its trunk. We wanted to preserve our evergreen, so we brought a large pair of garden shears to remedy the problem. When we reached inside the evergreen's branches, we were shocked to find that the two trees were fused together. There was no way to cut down the invasive tree without killing our evergreen. They were attached. One year later, both trees were dead. They were not healthy for each other.

Just as the evergreen and the other tree fused together in an unhealthy way, people can make unhealthy connections. Caregivers may be untrustworthy. Parents may be abusive or negligent. Even when the attachment isn't safe, our drive for connection can still fuse us to the people around us. What do those unhealthy or insecure attachments look like? Just as we discussed how healthy attachments look developmentally through a child's different stages, let's consider how unhealthy ones look developmentally.

The Terrified Baby

His arms are flailing and his back is arched. He isn't sleeping and only barely relaxes when he is in his caregiver's arms. He claws at his face, eyes, and arms. You have tried trimming his nails, swaddling him, and covering his hands with baby gloves. He scrunches up his face in anguish. You have changed the formula countless times and visited the doctor but no one has answers.

The Lethargic Baby

She barely makes eye contact. You have to wake her to feed her, and she is slow to eat even then. She doesn't cry when her diaper is dirty or when she wakes in the middle of the night. Others comment on how "good" she is. She will go to anyone and rarely makes a noise.

The Nervous Toddler

She jumps when you reach for her. She doesn't babble and hasn't formed words. She doesn't lean in when you hug her but refuses to leave your arms to go to a babysitter or friend.

The Over-Affectionate Preschooler

He climbs into the laps of every adult he meets. He smiles widely at everyone in the grocery store and asks strangers for candy, gum, or a hug. He tells his teacher he would like to go home to live with her and makes plans to get a new mommy just in case.

The Disagreeable School-Age Child

She will not do her homework. She will not load the dishwasher. She will not get in line at school after recess. She will not change her underwear. She will not brush her teeth. She will not agree that the sky is blue.

The Greedy Preteen

He takes more than his fair share at snack time. He changes the rules to a game he's playing with his friends. He takes his brother's sweatshirt and stuffs it into the bottom of his dresser, claiming it's his. He is unhappy with his birthday party, gifts, and cake, and wishes out loud for something different. He gets a new pair of shoes and immediately wants what the neighbor has.

The Disobedient Teen

She comes in late for curfew. She lies about where she was even though you saw her there. She will not complete chores or go to bed on time. She challenges every boundary and pushes against them with force. She claims that any consequences are someone else's fault.

The Overly Compliant Teen

He does everything you ask him and is always smiling. He makes peace with others and compromises on things that you know he feels strongly about. He gives in to others. He is easily pushed around. You ask him how he's doing but he assures you everything is fine. He claims he is not bothered by anything anyone around him is doing. He promises you that he is unaffected by his circumstances.

The Manipulative Teen

He claims that "everyone" else has something he doesn't, such as freedom, clothing, privileges. He twists the truth and blames others when he gets caught. He makes passive-aggressive statements that hurt but won't take responsibility for his words.

The Promiscuous Teen

She becomes attached to every person she comes in contact with. She may engage in a sexual relationship or she may race into a deep emotional relationship with people, including their extended families. When the friendship or romantic relationship ends, she quickly moves on to another relationship.

The Directionless Young Adult

This young adult may or may not enter college or the workforce, but has an inability to see anything he does through to conclusion. He blames his parents for his lack of direction. He berates them for not caring about him or making sure he has what he needs (even though they have done everything in their power to care for him). He never calls them except to place blame or ask for money. He often goes through friendships and dating relationships quickly because others become fed up with the self-centered behavior.

The Disconnected Marriage

He is the spouse who cannot connect, bend, compromise, or understand another point of view. He does not trust and cannot rest and enjoy his spouse. He may instigate arguments or downplay his own emotions, stuffing them inside. He may seem needy or he may push his spouse away.

The Disconnected Parent

This parent doesn't listen to their child. He seems distant and detached. He may not know how to respond if the child is hurt or sick. He may freeze in the face of trauma. He may seem self-indulgent or may have workaholic tendencies, putting other things above relationships.

The Codependent Parent

This parent may try to live through the experiences of her child. She may overschedule and overplan her child's life. This parent may cling to her child, preventing the child from maturing toward independence. She may treat her child as more of a friend.

How Personality Types Affect Attachment

When someone who has experienced disrupted attachment as a result of trauma grows into adulthood, we may see additional issues or characteristics develop:

The Person Who Is Easily Tricked or Manipulated

This person doesn't know when someone is trying to harm them. They may be described as gullible and too trusting. They don't know how to tell if someone is a good friend. Long ago, we cared for an older child through foster care who regularly entered into friendships with kids who took advantage of him, stole things from him, and then stopped talking to him when they had received all they wanted from this child. It was excruciating to watch.

The People Pleaser

This person may not stick up for himself in marriage, extended family, with neighbors, or at work. He may not identify or stand behind his own opinions for fear of losing relationships. A family we coached were parents to a young adult son who fit this description. He continually came to them brokenhearted because others made decisions for him that he didn't agree with. Yet he had no ability to speak up and give his input. The outcome was normally days of him dealing with depression or self-harm.

The Person with Lack of Self-Preservation

This person can't seem to assess the danger of a situation. She may find herself in dangerous situations without even trying. She may drive too fast, refuse to wear a seat belt, or engage in thrill-seeking activities. Recently, we coached a parent who was raising a child with this characteristic. The parent was distraught because her daughter was routinely getting into cars with strangers, most recently convicted of a felony, and continually sneaking out of the house to be with people who often ran into trouble with police.

The Isolated Person

This person does not seek out relationships. His idiosyncrasies may prevent him from eating at another person's house or having a flexible schedule. He may desire relationships but not know how to create them.

The Dangers to a Lack of Healthy Attachments

A lack of healthy attachments, or disrupted attachment, can be dangerous for many other reasons. When we don't have healthy attachments, finding ourselves in dangerous situations or relationships becomes a much greater possibility. It can create lowered defenses, vulnerability, isolation, and lack of accountability. Here are some additional reasons a lack of healthy attachment is dangerous as it relates to the children we are caring for.

High Risk for Sex Trafficking

According to the National Foster Youth Institute, 60 percent of all child sex-trafficking victims have histories in the child welfare system. In the United States, the FBI estimates that sex trafficking involves one hundred thousand children on a yearly basis. In 2013 alone, 60 percent of children recovered by FBI raids across the United States were from foster care or group homes. If you're doing the math, that's sixty thousand children from foster care or group-home environments. What's equally alarming is that experts have determined the average age for girls entering the sex-trade industry is only twelve years old. Children recovered by law enforcement, who were being prostituted, averaged just fourteen years of age.[2]

Inability to Decipher Whom to Trust and Not Trust

If you're caring for a child who has a trauma history, you may already see signs of this. Early on in our parenting journey (foster care in particular), we cared for several children about whom the case manager claimed that they "have no enemies" or "have never met a stranger." This became alarming to us because a child with no inhibitions would jump into the arms of strangers or ask to go home with people we had never met.

Superficial Relationships

Children who have experienced disrupted attachment can often enter into superficial or toxic relationships, with little or no ability to see that the relationship is not reciprocal. We have seen children meet kids and instantly refer to them as best friends. That was concerning, but our fears were fueled when the child would constantly be taken advantage of by another child who claimed to be their friend.

Constant Survival Behavior Mode

Many of us have parented children (teenagers in particular) who, out of disrupted attachment, exist in a state of survival mode. Their behaviors are often impulsive, belligerent, disrespectful, or manipulative. This retreat to the survival brain is a defense mechanism. Rational thinking and reasoning cannot take place in survival brain, which makes it difficult to form acceptable behaviors. Instead, their behaviors are fighting, threatening others, stealing, hoarding, and running away.

Developing Healthy Attachments to
Replace Unhealthy Ones

Unhealthy attachments put our kids on a path toward potential destruction. And that's scary to us, isn't it? Like any good and loving parent, we want to replace the unhealthy attachments with healthy ones. That starts by us committing to rebuild the attachment through intentional connection, trust, consistency, and time. We may know our home is safe. We may know we are safe. A child may not know those things. If attachment has been damaged or disrupted, the child will need you to rebuild that trust. We teach our children that we can be trusted when they know what to expect from us. Our children should feel confident of our reactions, our schedule, our tone, and our expectations.

Your children have the ability to heal from broken or disrupted attachment. And as a caregiver who is on the front lines, you also have the ability to heal. We believe in healing so deeply because, as people of faith, we have received the greatest healing of all. Our hope and healing come from a loving heavenly Father who has never left us and promises to heal our deepest wounds.

Rebuilding and healing is possible, but it takes time. We'll talk more specifically about how to rebuild those attachments in upcoming chapters.

What Now?

- For more information about how unhealthy attachments can be detrimental for children in foster care, read "Sex Trafficking" on the National Foster Youth Institute's site at https://www.nfyi.org/issues/sex-trafficking/.
- Journal or discuss with a friend:
  - Who are the top three people you are attached to?
  - Do you have a sense of belonging in your family?
  - Do you have a sense of purpose in your community?
  - Who are the top three people your child is attached to?
  - Does your child have a sense of belonging in your family?
  - Does your child have a sense of purpose in their community?
- Read *Attaching through Love, Hugs and Play: Simple Strategies to Help Build Connections with Your Child* by Deborah Gray.

Remember . . .

- *Attachment to a caregiver sets the expectation for other relationships.*

- *Healing happens within healthy relationships.*

- *Healthy attachments lay the foundation for resiliency and healing.*

CHAPTER 5

HOW TRAUMA DISRUPTS ATTACHMENT

When Sylvia was eleven months old, her mother died suddenly. Her mother valued self-led weaning, so when she died, Sylvia's main source of nourishment and comfort disappeared. With her primary attachment severed, Sylvia was left with feelings of uncertainty surrounding relationships and attachments. And the trauma she experienced disrupted her ability to form healthy attachments as she grew older.

In *The Primal Wound*, Nancy Newton Verrier describes this disrupted attachment like this: "What the child has missed is the security and serenity of oneness with the person who gave birth to him, a continuum of bonding from prenatal to postnatal life. This is a profound connection for which the adoptee forever yearns. It is the yearning which leaves him often feeling hopeless, helpless, empty, and alone."[1]

Healthy attachment to caregivers creates a measure to weigh other relationships against. Lack of healthy attachments lead to a scale that is off balance. Children who have entered into an adoptive or foster home have had their attachment to their first parents severed. They have experienced trauma. Remember that any type of trauma sends a signal to the brain that something is wrong. That signal sounds the alarm that overrides the prefrontal cortex, the thinking and logic part of the brain. According to Karyn Purvis, "If a child feels threatened, hungry, or tired, her primitive brain jumps in and takes over. Physically located in areas of the brain such as the amygdala, this primitive brain constantly monitors basic survival needs and behaves like a guard on patrol. When the primitive brain is on duty, more advanced areas of the brain—particularly those that handle higher learning, reasoning, and logic—get shut down."[2] We know that rational thinking, reasoning, and executive functioning happen in the prefrontal cortex, but did you know that attachment, bonding, and relationship building also take place there? If a person is functioning from their brain stem—the survival part that keeps them alive—they are not able to use the part of their brain that builds healthy attachments.

Trauma Disrupts Attachment When Trust Is Lost

When I (Kristin) was a kid, I was on the cross-country team. Before each race, runners from the away team walk the course so they know what to expect. I used to love that initial walk-through because it helped me visualize where I was going. I knew where I would need to slow down and save my strength right before the hills or where I could gain momentum on the long even stretches. During one race, I hit my groove and my body felt good. As I rounded a corner, building the strength to pass my opponents, I landed my right leg in a hole. I twisted my ankle, not badly, but enough to disrupt my flow. I shook my leg and rotated my ankle and then resumed my pace. But I never made up that lost time.

That unexpected hole disrupted my trajectory. My race wasn't the same after that. Trauma does the same thing. It is a bump in the road. Sometimes it is minor and we recover quickly, and sometimes the trauma changes our course entirely.

When I was running, I trusted that I knew the course, so my feet fell confidently along the path. When I fell into the hole, my trust in my path and myself was damaged. I ran with less assurance for the rest of the race. My new lack of confidence cost me precious speed. The same happens when our children lose trust in their caregivers and environment. A child may sleep well every night in the safety of their home but if that home catches on fire during the night, that child may have difficulty sleeping for years to come. The feeling of safety is now gone. Trauma causes a feeling of fear, a lack of trust.

Verrier describes the fear that children feel this way: "Many adoptees find it difficult to attach or allow closeness in relationships because of the fear that each new relationship, like the very first relationship, will not last."[3] Attachment happens when the brain is able to reason and remember, building on the trust that has been stored over a lifetime. But fear, or lack of trust, sends the brain into survival mode. When the brain is in survival mode, it cannot connect with the reasoning part of the brain and therefore attachment isn't possible during this time.

Survival Brain Disrupts Attachment

"It just doesn't make sense," one couple told us over their eight-year-old's confusing behavior. "We have given her everything she needs. We are with her when she is sad or angry. We try patiently to respond when she's melting down or lashing out. She has healthy meals, a good school, and a warm home. What more does she want?"

As they shared their story, it became clear that this child had simply not gained the trust needed to build a secure attachment. She has only been in their care for three years. They missed the first five years of her life, the crucial period when secure attachments to caregivers are formed. When they shared the timeline and the short period they had her in their care, her behavior made sense. She was in survival mode. And because of this, she was not able to connect to the fact that she now had caregivers who would provide for her, care for her, and love her. She needed more time and consistency than only three years could provide.

Attachment is based on trust, which is built on facts gathered by the rational brain. Trauma, however, overrides the rational brain and throws it into survival mode, which means attachment gets disrupted. A child who experiences chronic trauma is experiencing the overridden brain over and over. This child may be living in his survival brain and unable to override the survival brain instinct. Remember that the survival brain is concerned with only one thing: survival.

Recently, I (Mike) talked with a friend who was distraught over his fifteen-year-old son's behavior. His son had resorted to stealing almost every time he was out of their sight. He would steal from major retailers, convenience stores, classmates, his workplace, even neighbors and strangers. It had escalated to a potentially dangerous level (let alone, wildly illegal).

On a personal level, this child seemed to push my friend and his wife away. Their attempt to care for him was always met with a lack of trust (even after a decade of parenting him). Another interesting fact here was that my friend is well off financially. He and his wife live in a large suburban home and have the means to provide for all of their children. This child had access to anything he wanted, so why the compulsive stealing?

As my friend and I processed the issue, we walked back through this child's past. Turns out this child spent his early childhood malnourished before he was removed from his mother's care and placed in foster care. The first few foster homes were nothing short of bad experiences. Two different sets of caregivers were abusive and neglectful. By the time my friend's son came to his home, it was this child's fifth home. With this understanding, the compulsive stealing made sense. This child had experienced chronic trauma early on to such a degree that, even though a decade had passed since the bulk of his trauma took place, he was still living in a brain unable to move out of survival instinct, which meant he couldn't attach.

When a child enters the foster care system, they have just experienced an enormous trauma, the loss of their family and home. They may have experienced chronic trauma up to that point as well, such as neglect, hunger, housing insecurity, or abuse. The foster home may be a safe place, but it doesn't feel safe to the child. Everything around them feels uncertain and unfamiliar, which is like a warning signal. The caregiver is not their parent, the home doesn't feel right, dinner is at the wrong time, and the food tastes weird. They don't know if they should trust this new caregiver. Their need to survive feels overwhelming and causes them to be unable to think logically about all that is happening.

How Disrupted/Insecure Attachment Feels to a Child

When I (Kristin) was a teenager, I loved to go to haunted houses. I loved that feeling of uncertainty just before entering. I heard scary sounds and saw lights ahead but never knew what was coming. The haunted houses had temporary walls meant to disorient and confuse. Hands reached out from above and people dressed in gory costumes jumped out from every dark corner. I was filled with momentary terror. My heart raced, my hands felt clammy, and I may have tried to punch a creepy clown that came out of a dark closet. My body was reacting naturally to the fear. We were only inside a few minutes, and as we were chased away from the property by a chainsaw-wielding maniac, we dropped to the ground in fits of laughter. We *knew* we were safe. Our life experiences taught us that most places and people are safe. We could delight in a few jumps and scares because our logical brains told us that the fear would last only for a moment, and it was all for fun.

Children who live without secure attachments can feel like they are *living* in a haunted house, never knowing what lies around the next corner. Nadine was adopted at the age of four. In her early years, she was cared for by many caregivers, including her biological parents, friends, aunts and uncles, and foster parents. She was never able to form secure attachments to her caregivers because of neglect, abuse, and disruption of constantly being shifted from one caregiver to another. When she joined her adoptive family as a preschooler, she had already learned not to trust caregivers. At the age of eighteen, Nadine's brain still sounds the alarm whenever she feels discomfort, stress, uncertainty, or a memory of past trauma. Nadine had years' worth of proof that her family would protect and provide for her, but during times of stress, her brain switched back into survival mode, overriding her ability to recall the evidence that showed that families are safe and that relationships are valuable.

During the COVID-19 pandemic, Nadine's family stayed in quarantine in their small house. She was often angry with her family, lashing out at them for minor offenses. She refused to help with chores or join them for dinner. She claimed that her mom and dad were taking everything away from her and that there was nothing left to work toward. Her brain was on high alert because of the virus, and worry about school, friends, and loved ones. Though her family rationally explained the circumstance, and logically she would know the truth of it, because she was working out of survival brain, she was in a constant state of panic and hypervigilance. It played out in her family as looking self-centered and angry. For Nadine, disrupted and insecure attachment felt overwhelming.

How Disrupted/Insecure Attachment
Feels to the Caregiver

Before we became parents we dreamed of what parenting would be like. We imagined cradling our newborn in our arms while she curled her tiny body into us. We had visions of him reaching his little hand up to hold ours. We envisioned sharing the experience of Little League teams. We never doubted the role we would play in supporting our children through high school graduation, college move-in, wedding preparations, or raising families of their own. Though we didn't expect to be the center of their world, we wanted to be needed and included. So we were surprised when the baby screamed day and night turning his rigid body away from us. We were sad when our three-year-old refused to hold our hand. We were confused when we volunteered for our child's Little League baseball team, and he ignored us. We felt hurt when we were the last to know about the college acceptance or the pregnancy or the wedding we weren't invited to. Disrupted and insecure attachment feels confusing and disappointing to the caregiver.

We may tell ourselves, as parents, that given the trauma our children have endured, the emotions we feel around the disrupted and insecure attachment are invalid and that we should just get over ourselves. It's true that our job is to create stability and security for our children and expect nothing in return. However, it's also important to give ourselves grace and understanding. Humans thrive in connection. When we attach to our children naturally, we care for them unconditionally, even to the point of exhaustion. Just when we think we can't do one more midnight feeding, they smile at us and that reward pushes us forward to give more love and more care. We will do anything for our children without the expectation of getting something in return. But when they do show us love, it is a feeling like no other. We love this feeling of connectedness. When we don't experience that, because a child's ability to attach in healthy ways has been broken, we feel disappointed.

I (Mike) spent years struggling with what seemed like self-centered or narcissistic behaviors in some of our children. "Why is she so self-centered?" I would lament. "Why can't he see there are other people in this household, not just him?" These survival behaviors surrounding the disrupted attachment felt deeply hurtful and disturbing. In recent years, I've gained a new understanding of the driving force behind these behaviors. Verrier points out that "the severing of that connection between the adopted child and his birthmother causes a primal or narcissistic wound, which affects the adoptee's sense of Self and often manifests in a sense of loss, basic mistrust, anxiety and depression, emotional and/or behavioral problems, and difficulties in relationships with significant others."[4]

In other words, children who have experienced repeated traumatic experiences live in a bubble. The only person they can see in this bubble is themselves. It's how they've learned to survive (or cope), especially when it comes to relationships or a connection to others who care for them. The old adage "Looking out for number one" applies here.

Even though Verrier's words give us insight into what our children are experiencing, it still doesn't take away our hurt when our children behave out of disconnectedness. Disrupted or insecure attachment can leave us feeling uncertain and ill-equipped to parent well. Fortunately, when we remember that disrupted or insecure attachment is the root of their behaviors, that can empower us to work more intentionally toward helping them establish more secure attachments.

Why Lack of Attachment Feels Personal

Even though we feel compassion for all that our children have experienced, it's easy to take personally our children's behaviors or moments when we feel they've pushed us away. Many parents feel perplexed that children who have been in their care, some since infancy, push them away. It doesn't feel like the natural parent/child relationship they expected. That's because it isn't. It's hard *not* to take that personally, but we need to work hard to remember that what they are experiencing isn't about us. The relationship between an adoptive or foster parent and a child is formed by loss and trauma.

In order for us not to take personally their inability to attach to us, it helps us to remember that they *may not* remember or understand why they are behaving in certain ways. In the fall of 2013, the two of us were sitting in a special training session led by trauma expert Julie Alvarado. One of the biggest myths Julie dispelled was the belief that infants, in particular, do not remember the trauma they experienced in utero, or soon after entering the world as a newborn. We were surprised to learn that their brains and bodies captured the memory of their trauma even if they could not articulate it.

This makes sense, I (Mike) realized. When Kristin and I were fostering young children, we were often perplexed by their intense emotions. A case manager would usually fill us in on a few details from the child's past, but I would silently dismiss it, thinking, *But she's a baby. Babies don't remember.* I couldn't have been more wrong. Even though a person may not cognitively remember going through a traumatic experience, their body, *regardless of their age* when it happened, keeps track and records everything. So when we, as parents, take personally their inability to attach to us, it could be that, though they aren't aware of the origin, their bodies and minds are simply working out of survival mode.

It also helps to remember that once we receive these children into our homes, they do not become a blank slate, ready to start afresh and anew. We cannot expect any child who enters our home to belong to us or to be willing to be shaped by us. We all come into this world with a bit of who we will be already written into our hearts and minds.

Keep Your Head Up

Broken or disrupted attachment may take time to heal, but it is certainly possible. It's a step-by-step process. Picture it like getting yourself out of debt, or heading back to the gym after a long time to get in shape. You don't go to the gym for the first time and walk out in shape and feeling great. It takes work over time. Likewise, when you start living by a budget, you won't save an abundance of money and be financially free after just one month. It takes consistently paying down debt and saving money over several months, even years, to achieve this type of freedom.

The same applies to rebuilding a broken or disrupted attachment with your children. You must consistently show up for your child even when they push you away. You may have to "show up" for years, even decades. It took nearly ten years pursuing one of our children, who constantly pushed us away, until we saw the first signs of a healthy attachment. There is hope. It is possible.

————————— **What Now?** —————————

- Journal or discuss with a friend:
  - What is your first memory? How does your body feel when you think of that memory?
  - How do you feel when you are disconnected from those you love?
  - How do you think your child feels when they feel disconnected from you?
  - How do you think your child feels about the disconnect between them and their first parents?
  - What are three ways you can intentionally build connection this week with your child?
- Check out the Attachment Institute of New England (ww.attachmentnewengland.com/support) for more information on symptoms of attachment deficits.

Remember . . .

- *Trauma disrupts our natural attachment process.*
- *Don't take it personally when your child doesn't attach immediately to you.*
- *Healed attachment will take time and consistency.*

BUILDING THE FOUNDATION FOR HEALTHY ATTACHMENTS

Twenty-year-old Sasha is a healthy, balanced, responsible, and highly engaging young woman. She's studying premed. She's friendly, funny, and can make any person feel warm and welcomed. Yet her mother admitted to me (Mike), "Go back in time, ten years ago, and this is not the child you see before you now. She pushed us away constantly, pushed every boundary, and behaved very . . ." She paused to gather her thoughts. "Very survival like."

Sasha's parents adopted her from Russia when she was four. From the moment she arrived, she was determined to do the opposite of everything her parents told her to do. "Those first years were rough," her father said. "We had no idea what we were doing or how to do better."

Fortunately, a wise friend reminded them of the facts surrounding

Sasha's experience in an orphanage for those first four years of her life, when attachment to a caregiver was crucial. Their friend gave them resources to help them understand disrupted attachment and to learn strategies to help their daughter heal, which they devoured.

It was not a silver bullet. Sasha's parents had many sleepless nights, many exhausting and defeating days when they felt as though nothing they did was working. The one thing they knew: they needed to stay on the path of working to build a secure attachment to Sasha. By the time she graduated from high school, she was confident and strong. Her mother says she's a miracle— and she is. Her confidence and strength is in part because of parents who determined to create a secure foundation for her.

We must be willing to put time into our parenting relationships, not just for the first eighteen years, but for a lifetime. The work we put in now is building a foundation for our children to better develop the healthy attachments we long for them to have.

Elements That Create a Solid Foundation

If we want our children to create healthy attachments, which will serve them well and bring peace not only while they're in our care but throughout the rest of their lives, then there are four key steps we must take.

Be Patient

When I (Kristin) was little, I heard this phrase constantly: *Be patient.* I wanted to do everything immediately. If I wanted to make a craft, I hauled the art supplies out of the cupboard and spread them across the kitchen table. If I thought about playing with my friends, I was out the door and halfway around the block before considering the possibility that shoes might be necessary. As an adult, I am much the same. I jump at trying new things, meeting new people, or painting the bathroom a bold color. Most of the time, this isn't a problem and leads to a lot of fun adventures.

But foster and adoptive parenting isn't something we jump into. When Mike and I were new foster parents, we got the call to care for a three-year-old girl. I was so excited, I rushed to the store to buy her summer clothes, a bathing suit, crisp pink sheets for her toddler bed, and an assortment of sippy cups, toys, and hair accessories. I couldn't sleep that whole night. I lay awake thinking of all the fun things I would show her. I imagined taking her to the children's museum, the park, and the swimming pool. She and my daughter were already friends, so I was sure that would ease her transition into our home.

The moment I realized my error in thinking was the moment I buckled her into my minivan. Her eyes looked at me with terror. She wasn't thinking of the fun things we'd do. She wasn't dreaming of a home with plenty to eat and a backyard to play in. She was frozen with fear.

Parenting children who have experienced trauma requires patience. We must strive to understand our child's perspective *first*, then seek ways to help them feel secure. We cannot fast-track healing or attachment. Let's think of the previous scenario from the child's perspective. She experienced food and housing insecurity as well as emotional and physical neglect. She was separated from her mother and placed in a foster home with four other little girls. A few months later, she was transferred to our home. But it was via an empty parking lot. Her foster mom and I arranged the meeting at the request of the department of child services. We agreed on a time and then pulled our cars next to each other. We introduced ourselves and then moved the little girl and all her belongings to my car while she watched helplessly. Her two foster mothers hugged and cried while she stared, unsure if I was safe. Unsure if she was going to stay with me. Unsure if she would ever see her biological siblings, foster siblings, or her own mother again.

My job for years was not only to provide a safe environment and to love and nurture her, it was also to be patient with her. Part of the foundation for her security, attachment, and healing was laid brick by brick, experience by experience, year after year. I couldn't expect her to become whole and healthy on my time frame. I had to remember that she had to lead the way with her healing, and Mike and I had to be patient.

Build Trust

Mya is energetic and curious. But from her trauma history, she has carried a deep sense of insecurity and low view of herself. She constantly uses statements like, "I'm a loser," or "Nobody could ever love me." She often moves into a deep state of depression that lasts days when something doesn't go right. Her caregivers know that she witnessed and experienced domestic abuse. She heard the demeaning and degrading words her birth father said to her birth mother and to her. Those words embedded themselves deep within her memory. They cloud her view of what is truthful about her. She often asks her adoptive mother if the memories she has of her father abusing her and her mother are real, and if the things she heard him scream at her and her mother are true. Mya's mother speaks truthfully about the past, including many good things she knows about Mya's parents. For instance, Mya's mother is a talented artist like Mya, and her father has beautiful curly hair like Mya's. At eight years old she fully grasps what happened but is still grappling with what that means for her identity. Because of her caregiver's gentle honesty, Mya is slowly healing and forming a trusting and secure attachment with her new family.

In *The Connected Child*, Karyn Purvis writes, "Underneath everything you do with your children, you need to reduce their fears and convey the fundamental message that they are safe."[1] This begins and ends with building trust. Though we've already mentioned it, trust is a concept we will come back to over and over, because we may spend a lifetime building it.

Even after a child leaves your care and is out on their own, they will need constant reminders that you are trustworthy. One of our children came to live with us through foster care and was officially adopted four years later. However, her trust in us did not instantly arrive the moment we finalized the adoption. It took years of us meeting her basic needs, keeping her safe, and showing up for her in her moments of excitement, sorrow, anger, and celebration. The *first sign* that she had securely attached to us didn't arrive until nearly a decade later. She came to us when she needed help, she trusted us to care for her, and she hugged us when she felt better. We were over the moon! The feeling of secure attachment was worth the wait. Trust takes time. (This is why patience and trust go together.)

When building the foundation of trust, you build physical trust first. You meet your child's daily physical needs for nourishment, shelter, hygiene, clothing, and body safety—you provide plenty of food in the pantry, laundry, toothbrushing, and a safe and comfortable place to sleep. This is easy to do when a child is an infant, since they have to rely on you. But as a child grows, they may push back or resist allowing you to meet their needs. Continue to offer anyway. You can put a bandage on a child who has scraped their knee (yes, even if they are old enough to do it themselves). You can cook dinner at a regular dinner time (yes, even if the child refuses to eat). You can purchase their favorite shampoo or toothpaste (yes, even if they don't say thank you).

Meeting the need for emotional trust is equally important but a bit more abstract. To build the bricks of emotional trust, we must be aware of our child's emotional needs and work to create security around them. We build trust by respecting their privacy, especially around the details of their adoption or biological families. We always need to tell the truth, even the hard things. Our children must know we will not keep secrets or lie. We must respect their emotions and validate their feelings. We must be trustworthy.

Maintain Consistency

One of our foster sons came to live with us when he was just eleven months old. He had come from a history of neglect, which left him uneasy and often completely inconsolable. He cried day and night. If too many people were around, he burst into tears. If another adult tried to hold him, he sobbed. If he dropped his pacifier in the middle of the night, he screamed. The only thing that calmed him was for one of us to hold him. All the time. It took nearly two years of doing the same routine, day in and day out, to build trust. It was exhausting. But we knew that maintaining consistent caregivers, schedules, and routines changed everything for this little one. Eventually, he was able to separate from us for bits of time and then longer amounts. He was able to sleep in his own bed for a few hours and then eventually all night. He trusted that we would come back. Consistency, over time, is a game changer when it comes to forming a secure attachment. Here's how to establish consistency.

Establish a schedule. Establishing a schedule will not only help your family function at its best, it will help your child know what to expect each day. To the best of your ability, set regular wake-up times, bedtimes, and mealtimes. Even a newborn will recognize the consistent schedule. On weekends or holidays, keep the schedule much the same. You may have a child who likes to sleep in. That's okay! Still try to keep the schedule as close to the same as you can. Help your child by talking through any schedule changes that will happen on special days. For instance, if you planned a brunch for

Christmas instead of breakfast or lunch, talk to your child about the change and make adjustments if needed. Your child may be okay with a change of mealtime or they may need mealtime to stay the same despite the holiday. Offer breakfast at the usual time for this child and invite them to join in the brunch to have a snack.

Create attainable expectations. Create an environment that helps a child know what they can expect from you as well as your expectations for them. If you come home from work every day at 5:15, do your best to always come home at 5:15. If you create a bedtime routine of bath, book, and prayers, maintain this expectation. Furthermore, create attainable expectations for the child. In our house, everyone is expected to clear their plate after dinner, even the toddlers. Each age may do the task a little differently. Having attainable expectations for the child helps them feel they are a contributing member of the family. Caregivers can create go-to phrases around these expectations such as, *Mom and Dad always come home, Mom and Dad will always provide food,* or *The Berry family always clears our dishes after dinner.*

Routine is vital to a sense of security. Routine is different from schedule, in that routines can happen in and out of the regular schedule. For instance, when we get in the car, we buckle our seat belts, make sure everyone is safe, turn on the car, check our mirrors, and drive. This is a routine we do no matter what time of day or where we are going. If we have a bedtime routine, we can do the same routine whether we are home, camping, visiting family, or celebrating a holiday. Routines offer our children comfort. Within that comforting environment, they can access the parts of their brains that are wired for attachment.

Create traditions. Every Sunday we make a big meal and read our devotions as a family around the table. Every summer we throw a huge party for Mike's birthday, which falls on Independence Day. Every fall we carve pumpkins. Every year around the holidays, our family bakes cookies. These are traditions unique to our family. Our children know they are a part of something when we consistently engage in these activities.

Pursue Connection

We must always be in pursuit of connection with our children, especially when we're parenting those who have experienced disrupted or broken attachment early in their development. As Karen Purvis says, "Our children were harmed in relationship, and they will come to experience healing in relationship."[2] This healing happens through connection. Here are some ideas to actively pursue that connection.

Eye contact. Eye contact is a powerful human connection. However, eye contact can be uncomfortable for some. Some children will resist or even refuse. We must never demand that our children *maintain* eye contact with us. One thing we have found helpful is to ask our children to look at us, but not expect them to maintain the eye connection. For instance, we may be in the middle of a standoff and we ask, "Can I see your eyes please?" The child glances up at us, then quickly looks away. We don't demand they keep looking us in the eye. We say simply, "Thank you." That glance is enough to create a connection.

Find something you have in common. Our grandson and I (Kristin) love to go to the barn together and feed the animals. During this time, I listen to his voice, hold his hand, and scoop him into my arms on the long walk back to the house. Our youngest son and I love to tell stories. When I tuck him in at night, we create a story together. It might be a one-minute story or it might be twenty minutes, but it's all ours. Our oldest daughter and I like to get together for appetizers after the kids have gone to bed. It provides us with kid-free time to talk and share. Find something you and your child have in common and explore ways to experience those things together.

Eat together. There is something powerful about food. Throughout the Bible we read story after story of people sitting together to share a meal. When Jesus taught us to observe His death, He taught through the example of food. In 1 Corinthians 11:23–24, the apostle Paul wrote, "I received from the Lord what I also passed on to you: The Lord Jesus, on the night he was betrayed, took bread, and when he had given thanks, he broke it and said, 'This is my body, which is for you; do this in remembrance of me.'" Eat dinner together every night. Meet your child at school and share a sack lunch in your car. Meet for coffee or bake cookies together.

Take an active interest in your child. Several of our children are gaming enthusiasts. The two of us are *not* gamers. Two of our children talk nonstop about characters, as though they are real people. Their faces light up when they talk about gaming, and the two of us listen with interest. Do we understand everything they are talking about? Nope. Do we get so excited that we decide to give the game a try? Never. But we *are* interested in our children's perspectives, because we love our children and we want to be connected with them. So in the conversation not only will we listen, we will ask them questions about certain characters or levels or recent winnings. Find out what your child is interested in and connect with them through that.

Pay attention to subtle needs. One night, I (Mike) settled in for the evening in my favorite easy chair. On my lap was my favorite dessert. One of our children, who was sitting nearby, asked if I could get some dessert for her. It would be easy for me to say, "Sweetheart, you know where the refrigerator is. You can get your own dessert." However, we are working on more than merely helping our children become self-sufficient, we are working on building relationships. Pay attention to your child's subtle needs and requests. Even something as simple as, "Dad, could you get me some dessert?" can lead to a connection builder.

Building the Foundation with Time

Our twelve-year-old son has developed quite a talent for baking. I (Kristin) love the sweet smell that fills our house when he pops a cake into the oven. I can hardly wait for the timer to go off, and neither can he. I often have to remind him to use the oven mitts before pulling the piping hot pan from the oven. He's just so excited. He not only makes yummy cakes, he makes his own whipped icing. As the cake is cooling next to the bowl of fluffy cream and sugar, he can be tempted to jump ahead and finish the project before the cake has had a proper amount of time to cool. Anyone who has ever baked knows this can be a disastrous move. If you rush ahead with the frosting on a warm cake, the entire thing will melt into a mushy ball. Building a strong foundation for attachments is much the same as icing a cake. You have to take your time!

If you jump ahead to hugging your new teenage foster son without building trust, you may make him uncomfortable. If you swing your preschool-aged foster daughter up into the air and expect her to squeal with delight, you may terrify her instead. Take your time building the foundation first. When you do that, you'll find healthy attachments will result.

What Now?

- Journal or discuss with a friend:
  - How are you applying these four steps to your parenting strategy?
  - What are some family traditions you have? What traditions would you like to start?
  - What does your daily routine look like (morning, after school, bedtime)? If you do not have a routine, what is one thing you can establish today?

Remember . . .

- *Healthy attachments can happen.*
- *Healthy attachments take patience, consistency, and trust.*
- *Healthy attachments start with meeting needs.*

CHAPTER 7

UNDERSTANDING THE BEHAVIORS THAT HINDER SECURE ATTACHMENT

When I (Kristin) was ten, my family and I were playing in a river in Yellowstone National Park. Soon we were wading deeper in until we could lift our feet from the sandy bottom and swim. My parents stayed within arm's reach even though I was a strong swimmer. Suddenly I was swept into swiftly moving shallow water. I crashed against the rocks and began to scream, my hands clawing at the slippery riverbed beneath me. I flailed and yelled as tears streamed uncontrollably.

As I grew more frantic, my dad floated beside me. "That's enough," he said firmly. "Stop fighting. We're almost in calm water."

"I'm going to die!" I shouted.

"No, you aren't," he said. "We're safe."

He was right. In moments, we were in calm water again. He could see we were safe, but I couldn't. My behavior was wild, prickly, and unreasonable, but I was terrified!

Even though we can see our children are safe, they can act terrifyingly, wildly, prickly, and unreasonably. So they struggle to trust and attach to us.

So often we feel as if behavior is what hinders attachment. It can feel impossible to create a secure attachment when the other person pushes away, self-sabotages, or is unable to give and receive love. But be encouraged. You may not be able to control your child's behavior, but you can understand it. By understanding, you can position yourself more effectively as a parent and can work more effectively toward helping them attach.

How and Why Behaviors Hinder Attachment

For our children who have suffered trauma, typical everyday experiences can feel like being smack dab in harm's way, which can leave us feeling perplexed. We see an act of trust and affection as something beautiful and meaningful. We know that a hug is typically returned with a hug, but in our relationship a hug might be met with a push, a scream, or wide-eyed panic. Our child's survival behaviors seem out of place and unnecessary.

Consider the teenager who is lying on the sofa, scrolling through her phone, even chuckling at something she sees on Snapchat. Her mother asks in a friendly tone, "Hey, whatcha doing?"

"*Nothing!*" the girl snaps back.

The mother recoils. "Why are you talking to me like that?"

The daughter rolls her eyes. There was absolutely no reason for this response. But to this girl, everything feels like a threat, a confrontation. Because of her trauma history, she has conditioned herself to be on guard and defensive out of survival.

Survival behavior isn't about attachment, it's about survival. Here's how survival behaviors show themselves and can be confusing for us to navigate.

Survival Behaviors Are Prickly

When our foster son came to live with us at six months old, he screamed constantly. He clawed at his face, leaving deep scratches across his cheeks. If I (Kristin) tried to hold him close, he shrieked and turned his fists on me. All the loving things I instinctively attempted, he resisted. I wanted to love him, I wanted to feel love for him, but the more he behaved out of his fear, the more I felt pushed away. Because of his behaviors, I began to doubt myself and my ability to be a caregiver. Survival behaviors are prickly. They hinder attachment because they claw at the very one who is trying to provide them with safety.

Survival Behaviors Don't Make Sense

Kelly enjoys connecting with her children through activities. If the weather isn't a torrential rainstorm, frigid temperatures, or blistering heat, she's likely hiking with her children at a park, reading at the library, or heading off to the zoo. Kelly listens with patience and intentionally meets her children's needs with care. However, Kelly often finds herself exhausted by the end of the day. It isn't the activities that wear her thin. It's her eight-year-old son's arguments, temper tantrums, and incessant interruptions. Kelly doesn't understand why he acts the way he does.

Taken out of context, survival behaviors don't make sense. Fighting against an angry bear is understandable; fighting against a loving mother hinders the attachments that create security.

It Starts with the Brain and Their Emotional Regulation

That day in the water at Yellowstone, my (Kristin's) behavior stemmed from my brain's response to it, which caused my emotions to go into overdrive. When we look at out-of-control behavior, out-of-control emotions accompany it, which means our children are unable to emotionally regulate what's happening with them. This is called dysregulation.

Before we discuss dysregulation, let's look at the healthy aspect of emotional regulation. Regulation is our baseline. It's the feeling of being at peace and calm. This may be how we feel when we're sitting in our favorite chair, sipping a cup of coffee, wearing our favorite cozy socks. It may be when we're jogging through the park, filling our lungs with crisp air, and hitting our stride. It may be when we're at work and everything we do feels productive.

It's important to understand your emotional regulation first. Ask yourself: What do I feel like on my best day? What does my body feel like when I'm focused? How does my stomach feel? How does my brain feel? What does happy or contented feel like to me? If you can remember how those things feel in your body, you're headed in the right direction to understanding how your children are feeling.

Next, explore your child's baseline. Ask similar questions. What behaviors do I see as their baseline? What is my child's tone of voice? What is my child's posture? Is their body relaxed? Are hands resting open? How do they sit in a chair, walk, and move? What do I observe when they are working, thinking, and feeling at their best?

The opposite of this is dysregulation. Dysregulation is anything above or below our baseline. Remember, we all feel dysregulation at times. Dysregulation is not a judgment of a person's character, it is just a sign that we are existing above or below that emotional baseline. We may feel: anxious, silly, stressed, agitated, nervous, afraid, excited, unsure, confused, angry, tired, frustrated, sad. When

I (Kristin) feel anxious, my stomach feels sick. When I feel silly, I may laugh so hard that I can't catch my breath. For our children, dysregulation is their inability to regulate their emotions or responses to feelings, memories, or environment.

Ask yourself, how do I feel when I'm feeling above or below my baseline? Then consider, how do those emotions look on my child? He may clench his fists when he feels frustrated or rub his eyes vigorously. She may pace or use a baby tone when she feels insecure. When a child experiences emotional dysregulation, behavior becomes part of their response.

Behavior Is a Voice

Last summer, one of our teenagers began talking back to us and acting in a disrespectful way. I (Mike) was growing frustrated with him. One evening, after days of dealing with his behavior, while walking down the hall of our house, I passed the washing machine and dryer. On top of the dryer was his folded uniform shirt. In a few days, my teenager would start working his first actual job. That's when it hit me. His behavior was the manifestation of the nervous and anxious feelings that were swimming around in him. But he couldn't articulate them. The only way he knew how to express what he was feeling was through behavior.

We do a disservice to our children when we allow our relationship and attachment pursuits to be based strictly on their behavior. We must remember that something deeper is going on inside them— some dysregulation that causes the behavior to come out in the ways it does. It has an origin—it doesn't just simply appear out of nowhere. So we can't try to control the behavior only. That won't make for lasting change. In fact, we cannot address behavior until we first understand where the behavior is coming from. Behavior is a voice. It is a symptom or a reaction to something larger than the behavior itself.

When we think of trauma reactions, we often think of fight, flight, or freeze, but we don't often think of the many other ways a child can react. A child may also seem greedy, silly, quiet, affectionate, manipulative, angry, hypervigilant, charming, defiant, or lazy. Often parents, caregivers, and educators push back on this explanation, feeling justified that the child is actually just a bad kid. Or they may think that an overly affectionate child is clingy just because they like to be cuddled, failing to understand the reason underlying the behavior.

But since the behavior is a voice, the greedy child may have been starving when he was a baby. The silly child may use laughter to cover her insecurities. The quiet child may have learned to cope by pretending to be invisible. The child who is overly affectionate may be informally interviewing for a new mom or dad. To feel safe, the hypervigilant child may need things in precise order. The charming child may use the attention of others to overcome self-doubt. The defiant child may feel that obedience is a loss of control. The lazy child may be too overwhelmed, depressed, or anxious to make any steps forward.

Think of your child's behavior that worries you. Ask yourself, What does the behavior *really* mean? When we allow ourselves a new perspective, we parent differently. When we identify what the child needs, we can meet that need. Met needs lead to increased trust and ultimately to attachment. We can start with simple needs—hunger, discomfort, sleep. Ask yourself what your child needs, and if that behavior is natural. Maybe your newborn has a dirty diaper and needs it changed. If you meet that need but the behavior doesn't change—if the newborn has a clean diaper, a full belly, and gets a good night's sleep, but continues in an unnatural or disruptive behavior—then don't get frustrated or annoyed. Listen to the voice and dig deeper.

When Bad Behavior Is All You Can See

A few years ago, I (Mike) was flying into Los Angeles. I had a window seat, so I was able to see from the mountains all the way into the valley where LA is located. There's something about seeing where you've come from, where you currently are, and where you're headed, from thirty thousand feet above the earth, that gives you a deeper perspective of the world you live in. It's a view you can never see from the ground. On the ground you're too close. Only when you zoom out to thirty thousand feet can you see the full picture of your travel.

For foster and adoptive parents, this is also true. We need to zoom out for a moment on our circumstances with our children to gain a better perspective. When we see clearly their behaviors, we can respond in ways that actually help them. Much like gazing down from an airplane window, we need to zoom out, take a deep breath, and survey the entire landscape. This is something we cannot see clearly when our emotions draw us too close.

A few years after we began fostering, we cared for a ten-year-old who constantly behaved "badly." He melted down, pouted, or bolted out our door over the smallest things. He always fought us for control, even if there was nothing to control. The behavior made zero sense, and lasted for hours, even days. Similarly, you may be parenting a child who routinely acts out for no apparent reason. Some children may act as if they have no control of their bodies in public places. Some are aggressive toward siblings or caregivers. Often these behaviors happen when you're driving seventy miles an hour down an expressway, literally or figuratively. It's important to remember: *while our children may act out often, melt down, or severely misbehave in other ways, it's not always their fault.* Yes, their behaviors are "bad"—but this doesn't mean *they* are bad. Their behavior is a product of the trauma they've gone through. (Yes, even the children who have been in your home since they were born.) We may be too close to the circumstances to see what is really going on, and we need to zoom out to get the full perspective of the landscape.

Kristin and I have parented a child who can become verbally and physically aggressive at a moment's notice, going from peaceful to dangerous almost without warning. We have parented another child who becomes dysregulated quickly, loses control of his body, and suddenly moves from a quiet and calm demeanor to jumpy, fast talking, and agitated movements. A few years ago, we began asking ourselves three simple questions in those heated or tense moments to keep our perspective in the right place and to get to the origin of the bad behavior. This practice has helped us achieve the thirty-thousand-foot perspective on our children.

Our job is to find the truth of what is happening with our children *when* it's happening. It's important to ask these questions because it gives us the perspective we need to respond in a way that helps our children and builds a healthy attachment. Surveying the entire landscape of our children's lives (past, present, and future) can drastically change how we approach them, which then can drastically change the outcome of the tense moment. The good part is that we can ask these simple questions in a matter of seconds, right in the middle of what is happening.

Question 1: What Has Happened in This Child's Past?

Several years ago, one of our children began to raise his voice and verbally assault me (Mike), because he didn't like that we'd changed the schedule. It was time to head to a family gathering, and he wanted more time to play in the neighborhood. I'd given several warnings that we had to leave, beginning an hour before we needed to be in the car. When his tone became sharper and his volume increased, I found myself becoming agitated. As I fought the urge to lose my temper, a thought crossed my mind: *This is trauma behavior. It's not pure defiance.* The fact was, he was losing something. Even the loss of playing with other children was a trigger to something bigger.

My shoulders relaxed and my throat released the knot. My expression turned from a scowl to one of compassion. Instead of demanding he stop, I moved close to him, knelt in front of him, and said, "Listen, this get-together will only last a few hours. It will still be daylight when we get home. Why don't you ask your friends if you can play when you get home later today?"

We talked calmly, and he finally decided to ask his friends. Mind you, I've messed this up more times than I can count. But on this particular day, simply reminding myself where the behavior was coming from (what happened in the past) changed my entire approach, and ultimately de-escalated the situation.

Trauma history colors our perspective on everything around us. As caregivers, we must remember our child's past experiences to understand their current responses. So we ask ourselves, "What has happened in this child's past?" to remind us of that connection.

If you're fostering a child, chances are, you don't have the full scope of what they've been through or the situation they've come from, but you know this for sure: they have a trauma history. They've experienced deep loss and grief over their biological parent. They may have just lost the only home they've known. They had strangers tell them they couldn't live at home, then without a say or control, they had those strangers place them in another home with more strangers. And again they had no control over whose home they went to or how long they would stay. They may have experienced significant abuse or neglect, or they may have lived with a parent who battled an addiction, preventing them from caring properly for the child.

If you've adopted your child, or achieved some sort of permanency, you probably know more of their story. Simply asking yourself,

"What happened in the past?" when your child is experiencing emotional dysregulation helps to change your perspective. It also helps *you* stay regulated so you can respond calmly.

Question 2: What's Happening Now with This Child?

Several years ago, we noticed one of our children daily displaying unexplainable extremely aggressive, agitated behavior. It was the middle of the school year and everything seemed normal with our routine. For weeks we tried earlier bedtimes for fear it was a lack of sleep, changing diet, you name it. The behavior only escalated. Then it occurred to us: he was switching therapists after seeing the same one for two years. He was worried about meeting someone new and having to start all over. That would be a tough change for anyone, but for our child, it stirred up feelings of his time in multiple foster homes. Once we made the connection, we were able to intentionally support the transition to help our child feel more secure. This new therapist had a website that featured all of their clinician's photos and biographies, as well as a video tour of their facility. We watched the video with our child, looked at his therapist's picture, read her bio, then formulated questions he wanted to ask her. When it came time for his appointment, we went in with him. In fact, we did this for the first several appointments with her.

Keep in mind what is currently happening in your home. Is your child waiting for their adoption to be finalized? Did they just experience a difficult visit with a birth-family member? Are you fostering and a new placement just arrived? Have you had a change in the schedule or routine this week? Is school starting in a few days? Has the normal structure suddenly shifted?

Their behavior, whether silly, or aggressive, or defiant, can be a direct result of something currently happening around them that is causing them to feel afraid, anxious, or worried.

Question 3: What's About to Happen with This Child?

Last summer we were speaking at a family camp in North Dakota, and were thrilled that all of our kids could attend with us. Each morning we hosted a training session with the parents, while the children divided into small groups staffed with volunteers.

Just after breakfast on the first morning, we were headed to our different groups when one of our little ones started to behave erratically. He bounced all over the place, pestered his older brothers, talked back to us, and yelled at everyone around him. It was a full-blown defiance cocktail! Both Kristin and I had just about had enough. We were ready to go into shutdown mode (not particularly proud of that), when suddenly the thought crossed my mind, *What's about to happen with him?* It hit me. *He's about to walk into a group of kids he doesn't know, with a counselor he's barely met.* He was anxious. And this is how he articulated it.

"He's nervous," I quietly said to Kristin. "That's why he's behaving this way." She agreed.

Asking ourselves, "What's about to happen in the near future?" helped us re-gear how we interacted with him. Kristin took him by the hand and walked down a separate trail to talk things through. She reassured him that we would be right next door and that we'd let his counselor know that one of his coping skills was to be able to see us and say hi whenever he felt he needed to. The day ended up being successful for him. At first, he came in a handful of times to "check in" with us. But after seeing that we were right where we said we'd be, he stayed with his group and leader the rest of the day. Shifting our perspective that day changed everything for us. Often our children's behaviors are an indicator of something they are worried about or need but don't know how to articulate or appropriately ask. They need us to hear the voice of the behavior, figure out the real issue, and help them respond in a calm and thoughtful way.

We call that self-regulation, in which they are able to meet their own needs. We do this all day long as adults. We meet our own needs without even thinking about it. If we don't like the way our pants feel, we get a different pair of pants. If we feel tired, we go to bed. If we're hungry, we make food. If we're sad, we call a friend. This is the ultimate goal for our children, that they will be able to self-regulate as well.

Laying the Groundwork for Parenting through Difficult Behaviors

Some of our children won't display anxiety, aggression, agitation, or lack of impulse control. Some of our children come across in more subtle ways. All of us deal with anxiety, stress, and feeling overwhelmed, and we don't always do the best job of communicating our needs. So that realization can help us offer grace and patience to our children when they're in the midst of it.

It's important to note that your children's behaviors as a result of past trauma are not necessarily problems you can solve as much as they are windows into their need for security. These are opportunities to engage and set the stage for giving them secure attachments that they don't have to be afraid of or anxious over.

What Now?

- Journal or discuss with a friend:
  - What behaviors are you seeing that are a direct result of your child's trauma history? How have you reacted previously to them? What can you do to react differently?
  - Think of a recent meltdown with your child. If it were to happen again, how may surveying the trauma landscape change the outcome?
  - Armed with a clearer understanding of your child's trauma experience and subsequent behaviors, what is one thing you can do this week to support them well?

Remember . . .

- *Behavior is a voice.*
- *You can only change you.*
- *You have the power to understand your children and create an environment that promotes healing and attachment.*

IS IT BAD BEHAVIOR OR SOMETHING ELSE?

When we first became foster parents, we were surprised by our one-year-old's hypervigilance. He never took his eyes off us. I (Kristin) couldn't cook, take out the trash, or talk on the phone without him firmly wrapped around me. Every night I paced with him until he finally fell asleep in my arms. But when I tried to let him go, his body became rigid and he'd drop flat to the floor, hitting his head so hard I feared for his safety. Although he clung tight most of the time, he often wiggled free from my grasp at the most inopportune times, running into traffic or darting out the doors of the grocery store. He even escaped his car seat while we were traveling down the highway. If he was uncomfortable, hungry, overtired, or frustrated, he hit his head on the floor with surprising force and clawed at the faces of anyone who wasn't me. While I expected the nervous behavior for the first week or even the first month, he fluctuated from clinging to violent tantrums for more than a year.

A therapist helped us understand his extreme fear based on his exposure to trauma in his first family, then the loss of his first family, then the move to his first foster home, and then the loss of that family as he moved to our home. With the therapist's insight and help, we changed our perspective on what was going on and made a plan to keep him safe, meet his needs, and build the trust he needed for healing. We learned to ask ourselves, "What is happening? What just happened? What is about to happen?" We found that, in most situations, what we saw as "disobedient" behavior was actually an indication of something else.

This begs the question: How do you know the difference between disrespectful, defiant, dangerous, disobedient, manipulative, greedy, or annoying behavior versus behavior brought on by trauma? When we are confronted with our child doing something that feels like misbehavior, disobedience, or distracted, flighty actions, we need to figure out if this is them purposefully being that way or if they are acting in ways brought on by trauma.

Let's look at some ways our children may be "acting out" unintentionally.

Disrespect or Survival Instinct?

I (Kristin) was leading a youth program at a church I used to work at. One evening, the church hosted an event that took fifty older teenagers to a town festival, out to dinner, and then back to the church to stay overnight. We rolled into a diner around midnight, which was much later than we expected, but the kids were having fun, and it all seemed like a grand adventure. Kids poured out of the church vans and toward the restaurant. Everyone jammed into the waiting area, laughing loudly and joking around. It was chaos, but the good kind.

The hostess politely asked us to wait outside while some of the guests finished up so they could push together the tables. The adults moved the kids outdoors where most of them started a game of football in an empty lot next door.

One teenager was not having any of it. At first, she was angry with the other customers because they were taking too long and they had been "looking at us." I laughed, but when her eyes narrowed, I realized she wasn't kidding. She threatened to go back inside and tell the staff and the other customers what she thought about all of them. I tried to reason with her, and then distract her. Finally, I asked her to help me take everyone's orders, so we could just order all at once when we got back inside. I got everyone's attention and announced that they could each order two things. But she marched up to me, and with her face inches from mine, she demanded to have more than two things.

I had a choice to make. I could react to her anger and escalate the situation, assuming she was just being disrespectful, or I could ask myself what was really going on. A quick assessment told me that she was hungry, tired, and overwhelmed. It had been a long day, and the hunger and tiredness combined with the crowd and the unexpected change of plans were all making her feel out of control.

Instead of responding with anger, I said, "It seems like you feel really hungry and overwhelmed. What can I do to help?"

That was all it took. She stopped mid-rant. "I am," she said quietly. "I really want a burger, fries, and a milkshake."

I asked her to walk with me. "I can't let everyone get three things, but when the food comes out, I'll share my fries with you."

She started to get angry again, but stopped herself. "Can I go sit by the van?"

"Absolutely," I replied.

No one else knew what had happened, she got herself under control, and she ended up having a great time. She wasn't being disrespectful; she was overwhelmed.

As parents, when we want to get to the origin of our children's behavior, we must ask ourselves whether our children are being disrespectful or are responding out of survival brain.

Disobedience or Lack of Executive Functioning?

Lexi gets ready for middle school every day in a flurry of activity. She knows exactly what time she needs to leave to get to school on time. Since her mom drops her off on her way to work, Lexi also knows that when she's late, she makes her mom late. Her mom has told her repeatedly to be ready on time. But Lexi never is. Her mom has become increasingly frustrated with Lexi, because she feels Lexi is being intentionally disobedient.

But here's a typical morning for Lexi. She gets up, gets dressed, and heads downstairs, where she grabs her backpack. She puts on one shoe and just as she is about to grab the other shoe, she remembers that she needs her gym clothes. Hopping on one foot, she goes into the laundry room, drops her backpack, and begins to throw laundry out of the dryer onto the floor. She finds her gym shirt just as her mom notices the mess.

"Lexi!" her mom yells in exasperation.

Lexi looks up, confused. "Oh. Sorry, Mom." She scoops the mess back into the dryer, leaving a sock hanging out the door, and not realizing she threw her gym shirt back into the dryer. She enters the kitchen, grabs a piece of toast, and sees that she still has on only one shoe. She slides on the other shoe, leaving the laces untied, then notices her reflection in the hallway mirror. She pulls out her phone to take a selfie and then slips her earbuds into her ears.

"Lexi!" her mother shouts. "We need to go *now!*"

Lexi heads out the door before realizing she doesn't have her backpack. She races into the house, and for the next five minutes, she searches the family room, her bedroom, the bathroom, and then finds it in the laundry room. She is late to school again, her mom is late to work again, and they are both frustrated. On the drive, Lexi's mother lectures her about her tardiness and accuses Lexi of doing it on purpose out of disobedience.

Finally, after the lectures and arguments don't seem to make any difference in Lexi's morning behavior, Lexi's mother asks around for advice. She finds an online group of parents whose children all have executive-processing disorders due to Attention Deficit Hyperactivity Disorder, prenatal drug and alcohol exposure, or simply genetic predisposition. That's where she learns that Lexi isn't trying to be disobedient. She is struggling with her brain's executive-functioning abilities.

Lexi's mom gathers helpful resources from websites like understood.org and introduces Lexi to ways she can take ownership of creating systems within which she can function more effectively.

Lexi and her mom meet other families like theirs and Lexi feels less alone and less embarrassed by her struggle. She is able to talk with other kids like her and even gather her own ideas for staying organized. One of her favorites is writing her study notes for school using smelly markers. Another strategy is to color code her folders, calendar, and study sheets so she can see at a glance what she needs to do. Lexi isn't being disobedient; she lacks executive-functioning skills.

Executive functioning is how we, as human beings, get through our day, accomplish crucial tasks, keep ourselves organized, and stay productive. According to psychologists Joyce Cooper-Kahn and Laurie Dietzel, executive functioning is "a set of processes that all have to do with managing oneself and one's resources in order to achieve a goal. It is an umbrella term for the neurologically-based skills involving mental control and self-regulation." They also offer some examples:[1]

Inhibition

Cooper-Kahn and Dietzel define inhibition as "the ability to stop one's own behavior at the appropriate time, including stopping actions and thoughts. The flip side of inhibition is impulsivity; if you have weak ability to stop yourself from acting on your impulses, then you are 'impulsive.'" In other words, this child has little to no ability to stop saying or doing whatever comes to mind, at whatever time. Over our parenting journey, we have parented many children who either said or did things impulsively with no inhibition for consequences, surroundings, or what other people thought of them.

Shift

According to Cooper-Kahn and Dietzel, shift is "the ability to move freely from one situation to another and to think flexibly in order to respond appropriately to the situation." This defines foster or adopted children who find themselves in a tough situation but are unable to problem-solve. For instance, Rebecca is a smart and articulate twenty-one-year-old who can function, for the most part, normally. But when she discovers her car battery is dead and she has to leave for work at 8:00 a.m., she becomes stuck and unable to problem-solve her way through the situation.

Emotional Control

Cooper-Kahn and Dietzel define emotional control as "the ability to modulate emotional responses by bringing rational thought to bear on feelings." One time our son decided to impulsively build a tree fort from scraps of lumber he found from a recent room renovation. He had good intentions. He wanted to build a fort for himself and the neighborhood kids. When we realized what he was doing, we found sharp nails and screws strewn about the yard, and a few planks of wood half screwed into the trunk of a tree, with a rickety ladder leaning against it. To make matters worse, one of our neighbor's young sons was on the platform screwing more wood in. We were frightened for our child's and the other children's safety, and we reacted out of that emotion. But our son snapped back, "Why are you getting so mad at me?" He stomped into the house and slammed the door behind him. Our son displayed an inability to control his emotional response to others being upset over his actions.

Initiation

According to Cooper-Kahn and Dietzel, initiation is "the ability to begin a task or activity and to independently generate ideas, responses, or problem-solving strategies." Some friends have a grown daughter who has FASD (fetal alcohol spectrum disorder). Two weeks before Christmas Eve one year, they called to remind her when Christmas Eve service would begin at their church. She showed up at the end of the service. Later when they asked her about it, she told them she remembered talking about the service's start time, and she knew she needed to write it down on her calendar, but she never actually got around to doing it.

Working Memory

Here's how Cooper-Kahn and Dietzel define working memory: "The capacity to hold information in mind for the purpose of completing a task." If you are parenting a child with FASD, you know this is a common characteristic. One of our younger children can be given a task, understand the task, repeat the task details back to us, but then cannot complete the task. Several years ago, I (Mike) gave him the chore of taking out the trash. Yet I would find the trash bag sitting out on our sidewalk, halfway to the main trash bin. I was frustrated until I realized what was happening. As a solution, I began walking with him while he completed the task.

Planning/Organization

Cooper-Kahn and Dietzel define planning/organization as "the ability to manage current and future-oriented task demands." Eighteen-year-old Nicole was heading out on a road trip with her sister and dad. The day before, her dad communicated the details for their departure: "We need to have suitcases down to the car by 7:00 a.m. We need to leave by 7:15 to get to the airport in time to catch our flight." That night Nicole's sister packed her suitcase and brought it down to the front hallway. Nicole decided to watch a show on Netflix instead, insisting she would be ready to go on time. Yet at 6:45 the next morning, her dad had to wake her three different times before she started to move. When asked where her suitcase was, she had a blank look. She hadn't packed anything. From 7:00 until 7:10 a.m., she raced around grabbing her belongings, which were all over the floor of her room. She made it to the car by 7:20, and they zoomed off for the airport. As they merged onto the expressway, Nicole freaked out as she listed all the things she forgot (one of those being her passport). Nicole had an inability to plan and organize in a manner that would get her where she needed to be, with the items she needed for success.

Organization of Materials

According to Cooper-Kahn and Dietzel, organization of materials is "the ability to impose order on work, play, and storage spaces." I (Mike) have a high-functioning, high-achieving, and productive friend whose daughter was fired from her job at an office supply store. "They kept tasking her with organizing the back inventory," he told me. "To which I kept saying, 'That's not a good idea. Organization isn't your strength!'" His daughter, however, wouldn't tell her boss that she wasn't good at these assignments and to give her something else. Her boss grew frustrated with her as week after week he found the back inventory more disorganized than before.

Finally, he fired her. My friend's daughter had an inability to order herself and the store's inventory in a way that maximized organization.

Self-Monitoring

Cooper-Kahn and Dietzel define self-monitoring: "The ability to monitor one's own performance and to measure it against some standard of what is needed or expected." Back to the previous example. My friend discussed his daughter's firing with the supervisor in an effort to better help their daughter succeed in her next job. The supervisor shared that the continued inventory disorganization was just one piece of her firing. She could not grasp job tasks, and could not understand why her employer would grow frustrated when she did not perform well or hit the employee's standards. My friend's daughter had an inability to monitor her own performance and rise to the standard of her employer's expectations.

Think about your child's behaviors. Is it possible that instead of being disobedient, they are struggling with their executive-functioning abilities?

Bad Behavior or Diet?

Jordan was a rambunctious six-year-old who got in trouble at school almost every day. He wiggled during story time, bounced his legs under his desk, and got angered easily on the playground. He loved to read but could rarely sit still long enough to take the reading comprehension tests. Math came easily for him but he frequently had to sit in the hall during the math lesson because he kept shouting out answers and questions. At home, Jordan also had outbursts that made no sense. He sometimes couldn't sleep at night and stayed awake despite his parents' best efforts to relax him.

After years of this, Jordan's mom found a doctor who was willing to get to the root of the confusing behavior. The doctor tested Jordan for vitamin deficiencies and allergies and suggested an elimination diet to narrow down the foods he may be sensitive to. Jordan's parents eliminated the foods his doctor believed may be potential food sensitivities, such as those with high amounts of processed sugar, food dyes like Red 40 or Yellow 5, high-fructose corn syrup, wheat, dairy, citrus, egg whites, and gluten.

After a month, they began reintroducing the foods and monitored Jordan's response. Through this process they pinpointed the foods causing their son's impulsivity, anxiety, and inability to focus. The results were clear: foods with Red 40, Yellow 5, and high-fructose corn syrup were the culprits. When they removed those foods from his diet, Jordan's behavior and ability to focus drastically changed. With a simple shift in diet, they realized Jordan wasn't being disobedient, he was reacting to food that didn't meet his needs.

Dietary needs are not the same for everyone. As we've seen in recent years, more studies are being done on the effects of gluten, peanuts, dairy, and other food sources. While we may be feeding our children nutritionally sound and healthy food, their bodies may be receiving it in unhealthy and damaging ways.

Over the past fifteen years, we have personally discovered how much our children's diets play into behaviors. Allergies, sensitivities, sugar, water, vitamin deficiency, and the body's inability to process food dyes and chemicals have a profound effect on behaviors. What you think is disobedience may be an uncontrollable reaction to what your children are eating.

Bad Behavior or Sensory Need?

Saul has one pair of pants that he likes and refuses to wear any other pants—day after day. He prefers to spend his days wearing pajamas, socks, and a sweatshirt with the hood pulled over his head. He wears headphones every time he's out in public or when riding in the car with his large family. When he's in the store, he touches everything. He climbs under clothing racks and leaves fingerprints on jewelry counters. He licks his shirt and chews on his shirtsleeve. At night he piles every blanket and stuffed animal he can find on top of him. His parents want him to sit at the dinner table without his hoodie or noise-cancelling headphones, but he can't sit still without them. He tilts his chair and swings his legs. Teachers, day care providers, and other children are easily annoyed by Saul's behavior of touching things, making noise, and wiggling.

Saul's parents feel frustrated that he disobeys them by not stopping those behaviors. Finally, they talk to their pediatrician and get a recommendation for Saul to see an occupational therapist (OT). The OT gives them exercises to help Saul with his sensory-seeking behaviors. She also communicates with the school to create a plan for Saul to have body breaks throughout the day. Saul now has accommodations at school, such as fidgets, flexible seating, headphones, and comfortable clothing. Saul isn't being disobedient, he is sensory seeking.

Peyton gets angry and frustrated easily when he encounters any type of visual or auditory chaos. In the mornings, he becomes angry if anyone talks to him. If he walks into the kitchen and any cabinets are open, he closes them immediately and mumbles aggravation. He gags when mashed potatoes are served and can't even seem to take a bite. He hates the feel of jeans. Christmastime is especially problematic because of the lights and decorations. Adults in Peyton's life are often frustrated with him. They think he's being picky and unreasonable.

Peyton's therapist suggests that Peyton may be overly sensitive to sensory input. She encourages Peyton's parents to log his behaviors along with a list of observations about the environment at the time of the behaviors. Peyton's parents become aware of how he perceives sight, sound, smell, touch, and taste. They realize that he *is* overly sensitive to certain sensory input. Armed with this information, they work alongside the therapist, teachers, and other family members to create an environment that feels more comfortable for their son. Over time, Peyton learns to meet his own needs. He can remove himself politely from an environment that is too loud, or he can help decorate for Christmas with decorations that are simplistic and minimal. Peyton isn't exhibiting bad behavior; he is sensory avoidant.

As you evaluate your child's behavior, especially if their body is always moving, or they rarely take a breath between sentences, consider seeking out therapists who can help you work through your child's potential sensory needs.

Bad Behavior or Lack of Body Awareness?

Kaitlyn bounces down the hallway of her elementary school like a pinball. She knocks items off of her desk and hits her head when reaching down to retrieve them. She often gets hurt but takes a long time to recognize the extent of the injury. Recently, she cut her finger but didn't realize she was bleeding for ten more minutes until her teacher pointed it out. She knocks over her milk at lunchtime and misses the trash can with her lunch tray. She spins and bounces while waiting in line. She presses too hard with her pencil and often breaks her crayons. Her teachers accuse her of being careless and destructive, but she seems genuinely surprised to find her things broken.

Kaitlyn's teacher contacts the guidance counselor who observes her in the classroom. The guidance counselor requests an evaluation with the occupational therapist. With permission from Kaitlyn's mother, the OT puts together a plan at school for Kaitlyn to spend time in the resource room (a room equipped with accommodations for a variety of special needs) where each day she works on heavy lifting, swinging, and physical balance and coordination. Kaitlyn begins to recognize when her body needs more sensory input, and she and her teacher create a code word so Kaitlyn can request a body break. During this time, the teacher may give her books to return to the library or she may have Kaitlyn pull the wagon filled with lunches to the cafeteria. Kaitlyn isn't disobedient; she lacks body awareness.

If you identify with this, it may be important to set up a time to talk to your child's teacher, or resource team at school, to formulate a success plan for your child.

Bad Behavior or Triggered?

"I'm a bad kid and no one will ever love me!" eleven-year-old Cameron screamed at his father. "I hate you! I hate this family. I hope you all die. I'm going to kill myself." Cameron is typically a sweet, funny, kind, and hardworking kid. But occasionally his outbursts are verbally abusive to others and to himself. He shouts, screams, and damages property. Sometimes he puts his hands and feet on his peers and sometimes he makes threatening postures toward his siblings. Cameron is very worried that people won't like him and that he won't be good enough. He's afraid of not fitting in and of losing those he loves. He frequently pushes others away when they get too close. He takes correction and discipline personally and often internalizes the slightest correction as defeat. Sometimes he reacts sharply, which is often deemed as bad behavior. This is not the case.

Cameron's counselor works with him to uncover the root of his insecurities. Together they discover how his body feels when he remembers the bad things that have happened to him. Along with

Cameron's parents, they create a new narrative. They practice at home, saying good things out loud: "I'm a good kid and I do great things!" They shout together when they're feeling down. When Cameron feels overwhelmed or hopeless, he can now talk to his mom and dad about the feeling and use coping skills, such as reading, taking a warm bath, or wrapping up tightly in a blanket to feel secure and reassured. Cameron isn't disobedient; he is triggered by something that is happening or has happened to him.

As caregivers who are often exhausted from this type of behavior, it's easy to deem the behavior as just "bad." But more is happening. It's important that you investigate deeper to determine what is triggering the child.

Bad Behavior or Lack of Sleep?

Emma frequently doesn't sleep through the night. She loses focus at school and is quick to anger. She can't remember what she is supposed to be doing and also places a high demand on others. She moves her body in an agitated fashion and often seems to be trying to keep herself awake. She is unreasonable in her expectations of her friends. She often yells at people she loves or bursts into tears because she interprets their social cues as a rejection of her. She tends to lose friends because her behaviors are confusing and irrational. She talks back to her teacher and cries easily when she is reprimanded.

Emma's parents describe the ongoing behavior to her doctor. The doctor suspects that Emma isn't sleeping well. After a sleep study, they find that Emma isn't falling into a deep sleep at night. Armed with that information, they work together with Emma's therapist to create a soothing environment at night (no screens, light-blocking shades, a weighted blanket, and a box fan). The therapist creates strategies Emma can use to relax her body and teaches Emma's parents simple massage techniques to use as well. The doctor prescribes medication for when Emma still can't fall asleep. Emma's behavior turns around almost immediately. She occasionally has a tough night but she is now armed with the skills to help herself and with the knowledge to face her hard days with a little more understanding. Emma isn't disobedient; she's tired.

If this scenario sounds familiar, talk with your pediatrician about getting a sleep study. While you wait, take inventory of your child's diet, habits before bed, and any discomforts they may be feeling. Implement a few relaxing things into your nighttime routine, like a bubble bath, reading time, white noise, or a back rub.

Bad Behavior or a Teenager Growing Up?

Abby is excited to graduate high school soon. She has good friends, makes fairly good grades, and enjoys her part-time job after school. Lately, she's been pushing back against her curfew or boundaries around her phone, friends, or driving the car. She pushes back against things like saving money or planning for college. "Why do I even *have* to save money? I'm still in high school! I live at home. You're just trying to control me!" she often screams at her parents. They have been fighting a lot with each other but the arguments don't seem to go anywhere. Abby finally reveals one night that she is feeling confused and worried about growing up. She has a good conversation with her mom and dad and agrees that she needs the support. A few hours later, she is frustrated again and stomps to her room. Abby isn't disobedient; she is experiencing the process of breaking away that is necessary for all young adults.

It's likely that Abby has feelings of insecurity tied to remembering her separation from her first family. Abby's parents consult with their post-adoption counselor who helps them understand what might be going on from Abby's perspective. They talk with her about the things she might be feeling. She agrees that even she is often bewildered by her behaviors. They decide together to make a list of all the things Abby is doing to move toward adulthood. They check items off the list and celebrate every step forward. Abby begins to trust that her parents aren't trying to control her or make her go away. They just want to support her. Abby isn't being disobedient; she's growing up. In a situation where a teenager has a trauma history, the idea of leaving, or walking into something new, can bring up feelings of loss or grief. Though some breaking away is natural as a teenager is growing more independent, the seeming disobedient behaviors may stem from something deeper—the loss of stability or change.

If this sounds like your child, take steps to shift your role. Be intentional about pointing out successes they have on their own. Tell them how proud you are of them when they accomplish a task on their own or problem-solve with responsibility. Stand back when they make small mistakes to allow them to experience natural consequences.

Bad Behavior or Lack of Structure?

Aaron is excited for the summer. He struggles during the school year and can't wait to be lazy all day and just have fun. The first morning, he plays with Legos, reads books, watches television, goes to the park with his family, and does his chores. By the third morning, he exits his room disheveled and agitated. His mom tells him to get dressed because they have errands to run. Aaron drops to the floor in a tantrum and demands to stay in his pj's and play Legos. He runs into his room and throws his toys. He eventually returns to the kitchen dressed and ready to go. The errands take a few hours, and his mom doesn't have time to stop at the park as she had previously planned because of the earlier meltdown. Aaron feels confused and frustrated. He rocks back and forth in the back seat and calls his mother names. Aaron's mom and dad realize their child thrives in structure. That night they create a schedule for the summer days. It isn't rigid but it does provide an outline for how each day will go and what Aaron can expect. They state their simple expectations for their son such as getting dressed and making his bed. They also outline what their son can expect from them; a later bedtime of 9:00 p.m. and time outside every afternoon. Aaron isn't being disobedient; he lacks structure.

All children need structure to thrive. If you have experienced the same circumstances with your children, take a deeper look at structure and make this part of your days with them.

Bad Behavior or Fear?

Jacey joined her foster home one week ago. She likes them, and they seem nice. She especially likes a corner of the family room that has a beanbag chair and a bookshelf. She likes to get a blanket and read books in the chair. One day she is curled in the chair reading when she hears a commotion. The family is running through the house laughing and chasing one another. She is so startled that she doesn't realize they are smiling. The father picks up one of the children and throws him over his shoulder.

Before Jacey can think about what she's doing, she leaps up and starts throwing books at the father. She is screaming as tears pour from her eyes. She swears and stomps her feet. The father is so shocked, he puts the other child down and sends him to another room. Everyone is confused. For the family, a happy time has just been interrupted by a violent outburst.

For Jacey, something else is going on. After talking to the caseworker, the parents realize it is likely that Jacey experienced domestic violence in her home and that she is nervous about potential violence. She had frequent outbursts at school, on the playground, and in her former foster home. Jacey's foster mom and dad begin taking her to a trusted counselor who has experience working with people who have been exposed to trauma. They also modify their own behavior at home. They stay mindful of their tone of voice and do their best to refrain from making sudden movements or anything that may seem threatening. If they scare Jacey by accident, they apologize and help her create a plan for when things seem overwhelming. Jacey likes to go to the reading corner alone when things feel out of control. Her foster parents agree that if she is in the reading corner, they will give her space until she calms down. Jacey isn't being disobedient; she is afraid.

Fear is something that can live for a long time, even forever, in your children's psyche and it often manifests itself through behavior. Before you react to what is actually fear, take time to change your tone or body language and reassure your child. This response can bring a sense of calm and peace much quicker.

It's easy to misinterpret a trauma response, or survival behaviors, for bad behaviors. Thankfully, through adequate management, we can repair broken attachment as we learn to parent differently.

What Now?

- Journal or discuss with a friend:
  - Identify a concerning behavior in a child you are caring for. What does the behavior look like to outsiders? What clues is the behavior giving you? What happened in the past? What is currently happening? What is about to happen?

Remember . . .

- *We must be curious learners with our children.*
- *We must dig deeper to find the root of the behavior.*
- *What often looks like disobedience or bad behavior is actually something else.*

CHAPTER 9

THE CAREGIVER IS
THE DETECTIVE

Last year, our son was chasing his puppy through the backyard when he tripped and slid across a piece of broken fence.
His hand caught on a nail and sliced open his palm. We cleaned
the wound, but the cut kept bleeding. We had a choice to make:
we could wrap the cut and hope for the best or take him to the
emergency room to have a doctor x-ray the hand, clean the
wound, give him a tetanus shot, and stitch him back together.
We chose the latter. We realized that by treating only the surface
of the wound, we might miss an injury or infection that could
cause our son lifelong damage. Behaviors are much the same.

As caregivers, we see concerning behaviors and we want to know
what to do. We may try to fix the behavior at a surface level but
find our methods are like putting a bandage on a gaping wound.
After trying time-outs, grounding, yelling, and pleading, the behavior that first alerted us to a problem only gets worse. Something
deeper is going on.

A change for the best in our child's behavior, which paves the way
for secure attachments, comes only when we "hear" that behavior as

a voice calling out from somewhere deeper. The child doesn't know or understand, so they need us to help them figure it out. Since we often don't know there's a problem until we see the behavior, not only do our children need us to be their caretakers and parents, but they need us to act as detectives as well.

Finding Their Secret Passageways

One evening at Christmastime, after a full day of fun, our family decided to have a movie night and watch *Santa Claus: The Movie*. Each child bounced into the room clothed in their cozy pajamas with bowls of warm popcorn in hand. Suddenly one of our children escalated out of control. The movie, which we'd all agreed on, wasn't good enough. The popcorn wasn't what he wanted. The room was too cold. The complaints were one thing, the sudden aggression was another. Instead of stomping out of the room and calming down, which he wasn't able to do on his own, he threw pillows at his siblings, kicked the coffee table, and called others mean names.

Kristin and I stood dumbfounded. We'd all had a great day, we thought. Where did this come from? What happened? Who said what? Did someone aggravate things? Did we miss something? What could we have done differently?

As we worked to sort things out, it suddenly hit me: *This behavior has nothing to do with anything happening in this moment. It's bigger than that.* And in fact, it was.

He was triggered by the lights, Christmas music, and activities, which reminded him of the deep loss he experienced as a youngster around Christmastime. This holiday season was one big reminder of what this child no longer had.

Simply knowing our child's triggers is a tool that can change everything for us. That night was the beginning of a deeper understanding of our son. With that understanding came the drive to respond to his behaviors by creating a safe place for him to process all the parts of his past.

When I (Kristin) was a kid, I loved the *Scooby-Doo, Where Are You!* cartoons. They're about a group of friends and a dog—Scooby-Doo—who solve mysteries. Someone or something scary is always going on, and the team needs to solve the crime, rescue a victim, and uncover the person behind it all. Spoiler alert, there is never actually a monster or ghost to blame. The climax of each thirty-minute episode is when one of the teens pulls the mask off and uncovers someone we never thought would be a criminal.

Playing detective with our kids is a little like a *Scooby-Doo* episode. We might think we know what's going on. We may have a child who is stealing, hoarding food, bedwetting, or running away. Other people, maybe even our pediatrician, give us advice on how to handle the child. We hear things like, "Create a bedtime routine," or "What that kid really needs is a swift swat to the behind." We can sigh and feel isolated or we can play detective. There are always clues to what is going on beneath the surface. It is our job to uncover the mystery.

Starting Your Detective Work

Years ago, every week, the two of us watched New York City's finest solve an entire crime (with DNA evidence and everything) in one hour on the television show *Law & Order: Special Victims Unit.* We learned that a good detective never takes the crime scene at face value. A good detective starts at the beginning, with the original incident, and asks questions, taking nothing for granted. From there, they take steps back, until they can see the circumstances with more clarity.

To uncover what's going on with our children, we need to take on the role of detective. A good detective never ends an investigation before exploring all possibilities. A good detective asks the questions no one is asking. From our children's initial behaviors, we must zoom out and ask bigger questions, and investigate in detail, exploring all possibilities. To help us do that, let's revisit the three "trauma landscape" questions we discussed in chapter 7 and then let's add a fourth question. As a refresher, the three questions are: *What happened in the past? What is currently happening? What is about to happen?* And to these three, let's add: *What can I do?*

Rather than take their behaviors at face value, when we see a concerning behavior, we step back, zoom out in our minds, and survey the landscape—the past, the present, and the future. Then we take it one step further. We ask ourselves what we can do. Here are some steps to help us do our detective work well.

Observe Your Child

When our child was in second grade, his frustrated teacher called us nearly every day at his wits' end with our child who wouldn't sit in his chair or listen at story time and who would continually talk back in class. I (Kristin) was confused. I've raised a lot of kids, and this was not one I was ever worried about in school.

This child was polite, hardworking, and organized. I finally went to the classroom to observe a typical day. I hadn't made it five feet into the room when I realized exactly what was going on. Posters covered every inch of the walls. Coats were not in the cubbies, backpacks were strewn around the classroom, and half-finished projects lay all over desks and the floor.

I found my son's desk, neat and tidy, and I pulled out his chair and sat to observe the lesson going on in the front of the classroom. The children were unfocused, and the teacher encouraged them to listen but didn't stop them from interrupting or having side conversations. By observing the environment, I quickly had an answer for my child's out-of-sorts behavior.

When you observe your child giving you a clue to something deeper, ask yourself, "What are my child's five senses experiencing?"

For touch, ask yourself such questions as:
What is touching my child?
What do his or her clothes feel like?
What is the temperature?
Did we use a different laundry detergent?
Is he or she physically in some pain or discomfort?

For taste:
Is the child eating something that may have triggered a memory or a reaction?

For smell:
Does something smell different in our home right now?

For sight:
What is going on visually?
Is there a lot of visual chaos or lack of visual stimulation?
Are there blinking lights? Bright sun?
Is the room too dimly lit?
Are we watching something on television that reminds the child of something?

For sound:
Is there a lot of auditory activity going on?
Is the sound loud, soft, shrill?
Are we listening to a song, movie, or television show that brings up memories and feelings for our child?

Then consider: What is going on in the body? Observe how your child's body is moving. Are they lethargic or energetic? Are they sensory seeking or sensory avoiding?

What are their eyes doing? Are they darting around or fixed on something?

What are your child's hands doing? Are they clenched in fists or resting at their sides? Are they rubbing their eyes? Are arms wrapped around their body? Are they pulling or twirling hair?

What does your child's breathing look like? Are they breathing rapidly or calmly and evenly?

What is going on in your child's environment?

Listen, Ask, Offer, Listen

We need to listen, ask, offer, and listen some more. But let's just be honest—this may be hard to do. When our child is melting down, angry with us, or pushing us away, we can be tempted to react first. Caregivers often feel pressured to have all the answers. We must stop ourselves from responding first, and instead open our ears to listen. Our children need to feel they are worthy of being listened to, and they will give us clues if we just listen. When they use their words to communicate feelings, insecurities, memories, and fears, they need caregivers to listen without interruption or judgment. When our children feel they are not heard, behaviors escalate.

As adults, we give ourselves permission to think, feel, and share. Do our children have the same permission? We help them by asking simple questions: what, when, how, where? We dig deeper when we ask things like, "What's going on?" or "How did that make you feel?" or "When did you start feeling like this?" Only after we have listened completely to our child can we offer our perspective. We may say something like, "I wonder if you may be feeling afraid," or "Do you think you might be feeling anxious?" or

"I see that you're angry. Do you think you might be remembering a time when you felt that way before?" We might be wrong and that's okay. But at least we're offering possibilities that help our children continue to process their emotions.

Then we listen again, without interruption or judgment. Creating this trusted space gives us a greater insight into what is going on and helps them feel secure.

Document Observations

Recently I (Mike) was speaking at a training event when a young mom, who had been fostering a child for a little more than a year, said: "I'm confused by my child's behavior in public. Every week we travel to Walmart to get groceries. Everything is fine for the morning and during the drive into town, but after only a few minutes in the store, he loses it. He's out of control the rest of the day. What's going on with him?"

She'd already identified the trigger, Walmart, but I encouraged her to dig deeper: What sensory input do you observe there? What time of day are you shopping? What is your child's demeanor before and after a visit there?

I encouraged her to document her findings to help her discover the triggering experience. She may need to avoid the store altogether. She may find that preparing her child ahead of time with a snack, conversation, and a toy does the trick. She may find that by initiating the conversation with the child, she opens the door to a memory he hasn't even realized was bothering him.

It's important to document everything. You can use a small notebook you carry with you, the notepad on your phone, or an email exchange between you and your spouse, friend, therapist, doctor, teacher, or caseworker. The key to keeping a log is detail. Note the date and time the behavior is happening. Note what is happening in the environment. Document the circumstances in which those behaviors are happening. Is there a pattern? Take note of certain smells, colors, people groups, areas of the city you are in, time of year, and so on. What did your child eat that day? Who did your child see? What did you watch on television? Even the most mundane detail can lead to a discovery.

A few weeks ago, one of our children was struggling with dysregulation. This child was out of sorts at school, at home, in the car, with friends. No matter the situation, he was frustrated, irritable, unreasonable, overly silly, and tearful. We were becoming frustrated and irritable too!

We decided it was time to play detective. We asked ourselves about the child's physical needs. Was he getting enough sleep? What was he eating and drinking? Had anything changed in the environment around him? Was he sick or hurting in any way?

We considered his diet and began to investigate the food in our home, at school, and at his friend's house where he spent time. We asked ourselves if anything had changed in our diet, such as eating a different brand of cereal. We looked back over the calendar to see if we'd been eating out more often. We checked labels and looked for foods that we know he has a sensitivity to, in case we were missing an ingredient we hadn't discovered.

Then we investigated the amount of sleep he'd been getting. We asked ourselves what time he was going to bed each night and what time was he falling asleep. Was he having trouble sleeping? What was the environment like in his room? Was it dark enough, warm enough, too warm? Had he been waking up a lot in the middle of the night? Was he complaining of having to go to the bathroom a lot or having bad dreams?

Then we measured the amount of water he was drinking. Was he taking a water bottle with him to school? Had he been drinking water with dinner each night or was he skipping out on hydration in favor of snacks?

Next we asked ourselves if there were any issues with felt safety. Felt safety may not seem to fall into the category of physical needs, but we thought it was important to address. Was our child feeling safe in the home and at school? Were there any changes in our environment that might make him feel unsafe—such as a change of bedroom, a new family member, or an outside event, such as war or natural disaster?

After some investigation, we found out he'd been buying lunch at school and getting the milk as well. He has a milk sensitivity, but the school didn't recognize this. He was trying to put the milk back, but the lady who served the food was insistent that he take a carton. Once the milk was on his tray, he drank it. (He loves milk, poor kid!) The milk was making him feel agitated, which was leading to behavior that got him in trouble at school. He was waking up at all hours of the night and climbing into our bed. We knew he wasn't getting a lot of sleep.

With the tools of knowledge in our hands, we called the school and blocked dairy on his lunch account. We adjusted his nighttime schedule to allow for more time for him to fall asleep. The reset was just what he needed. The change was incredible. We could have treated the behavior with punishments, medications, or bribes, but we took time to look for the clues.

Help Your Child Play Detective

Up until our son was four, he hated certain pants. He cried if we tried to put him in a pair of jeans. If we even thought about making him wear dress pants, he melted down. He stood stiff as a board when wearing fabric that wasn't soft and stretchy. He seemed more at peace and relaxed in sweatpants or pajama bottoms. We began to help him observe the same things in himself. He described how certain fabric made him feel, then he explained what fabric felt good on his skin. With that new self-understanding, he was able to go to the store with us and choose pants that met the sensory requirements he had and the "acceptable for public" requirements that we had.

We must empower our children to understand themselves. We must pass the skill on to them so they are able to observe themselves, investigate on a deeper level, and one day meet their own needs when they are experiencing something that prompts unwanted behaviors.

Begin by using feelings language in your everyday life. Children will learn to understand their own feelings when they hear and see their caregivers use self-awareness. This can be as simple as saying, "Oh no, I'm so frustrated. I was about to make dinner and I accidentally broke a plate. I'm worried about getting cut. I'm feeling angry with myself but I know it was just an accident." Talking through our emotions out loud can feel silly at first, but this exercise is a necessary practice when working with children who cannot identify their own emotions. Slowing down our own reaction time and talking it through can be an invaluable experience for ourselves as well as for our children.

We then teach our children to understand their own bodies by talking about the feelings our bodies feel. We want to start doing this when our child is feeling calm. We can ask them a question like, "Tell me about a time you felt angry." As the child shares their experience, help them to dig deeper. "Where in your body did you feel angry?" and "What does the anger feel like in your tummy?" The more your children are able to identify their own feelings, the more likely they are to attach the root feeling to the behavior. When your children become detectives themselves, they can create environments and experiences that help them become successful. They can manage uncomfortable situations in a healthy and productive way.

Build Your Child's Emotional Language (And Your Own)

Emotional language is simply the words we help our children find and use when their emotions are escalating to describe how they're feeling, thinking, or processing. Emotional language may be words like *scared, angry, frustrated, worried, stressed, overwhelmed, annoyed, agitated, lonely, depressed, sad, mad,* or *anxious.* To help our children build their emotional language, it begins with us asking such questions as:

How do you feel?
Why do you think you are feeling this way?
Where in your body are you feeling this way? (Have them point or draw a picture, which we'll talk about more in a moment.)
What happened before you started to feel this way?
Is your brain saying something to you right now?
What do you think is making you feel _____ (fill in the adjective)?
Could you use a few words to tell me how you feel right now?

We must give our children permission to express how they think and feel. This permission will help them to identify the cause of the feelings of dysregulation we are seeing.

Your overall goal with helping your child build emotional language is to eventually lead them to express feeling statements on their own with little to no prompting from you, the caregiver. Here are some examples:

"I feel angry because . . ."
"I'm sad about . . ."
"I'm worried because . . ."
"This makes me angry because . . ."
"I'm frustrated over . . ."
"I'm annoyed about . . ."

The greater the permission given to express without fear of judgment or shutdown, the more you will hear statements like the examples above. Be cautious with the child who internalizes and never expresses (this can be survival brain activity). Create an environment that encourages expression of feelings and thoughts. Practice showing your child that you are strong enough to carry their feelings, emotions, memories, and thoughts with them.

A few years ago, one of our children's therapists had our child lie on a big piece of butcher paper. She traced around his entire body on the paper. Then they made a list of the emotions he often experiences. After they compiled the list, she asked him to use a marker and put a dot on the areas where he felt those emotions. They were able to identify the emotions, what caused him to feel these emotions, and where he actually felt them. Interestingly, he pinpointed a lot of dots on his stomach, especially when he felt nervous or anxious. He also placed dots on his chest and neck because he felt like his neck and shoulders were restricted when he was upset.

Our bodies are powerful communication agents that tell us how we're feeling, why we're feeling this way, and where the emotions are originating. We just have to listen.

Trial and Error

Acting as a detective means trying out many scenarios and solutions before settling on an accurate one. We may think our child is triggered by a trip to the grocery store only to find that the child is actually triggered by driving past the courthouse since it is the last place the child saw his mother. We can adjust our drive to the grocery store accordingly. We would never have come to that conclusion if not for trial and error.

Our daughter loves to celebrate her adoption day, unless she doesn't want to celebrate her adoption day. For us, it's a confusing time of year. She feels a variety of emotions: the loss of first family, the joy of her second family. The grief over leaving her family behind and the relief she felt when she was no longer in foster care. Some years, she can't wait to celebrate and some years she wants nothing to do with observing the day. Our job is to take our cues from her. We tried all kinds of things before realizing that we needed to trust her to decide how to observe the day and be available to support or celebrate as needed.

In the past, we have completely missed the mark with understanding and supporting our children well. Unfortunately, we will mess up again, probably often. When we misinterpret a behavior, we must apologize. When we punish without seeking understanding, we must make amends. When we lose our children's trust, we must take steps toward healing. It isn't too late to build security with our children through the simple act of apologizing.

It's going to take a lot of trial and error, so don't feel discouraged if you don't catch on to the clues correctly every time. Just keep at it. When you don't get it right, make amends. And when you do get it right, celebrate that you've brought your child closer to healing.

What Now?

- Journal or discuss with a friend:
  - What are some observations you've made about your child's circumstances surrounding a troubling behavior?
  - If your child isn't sleeping through the night or is throwing a tantrum every Saturday evening, answer the questions: Who? What? When? Where? Why? How?

Remember...

- *Our job as caregivers is to be the detective.*
- *Use the five senses in your observations.*
- *We are obligated to empower our children to be curious about their bodies and feelings.*

CHAPTER 10

PREVENTION AND INTERVENTION

When a friend brought up the idea of foster care to Ben and Lacy, they jumped in immediately. While they kept their focus on caring for a child temporarily while biological parents worked to heal and restore, two siblings they were caring for moved to adoption. Ben and Lacy agreed, without question, to become their forever family. At the time, Fiona was five, and Steven was three. For the first few years, everything was peaceful. But as Fiona grew closer to the preteen years, she became increasingly violent and often physically attacked Lacy. The older Fiona became, the taller and stronger she grew. Admittedly, Lacy and Ben didn't help matters by often reacting harshly to Fiona when she became dysregulated.

As Fiona approached her thirteenth birthday, Ben and Lacy sought out the services of a well-known trauma-trained therapist in their area named Sarah. During their first appointment (without Fiona), Sarah listened and documented as Ben and Lacy shared every detail of the past eight years caring for their daughter. After an hour and a half, she handed them a card for their next appointment and walked them out to her lobby. A week later, Sarah scooted her chair close to Ben and Lacy, reached for their hands, and looked them in the eyes. "Folks, first I want to say how sorry I am for what you have been dealing with over the past several years. It's never easy to step into the messy stories of children who have gone through trauma, but you're doing it, despite the hard days. So where do you go from here? What can you do to help Fiona?"

She then said something that resonated deeply with both Ben and Lacy. "I know you understand that her behavior comes from the trauma she went through long ago. But trying to modify or fix her behaviors is not the solution."

Over the next months, Sarah taught them how to both prevent Fiona's behaviors from escalating out of control and to intervene if they found themselves in a situation that was already out of control.

It's one thing to have a basis of understanding when it comes to behaviors that result from trauma, but it's another thing to manage a child's emotions in a real-life setting. Two crucial areas of behavior management can help us: *prevention* and *intervention*.

Prevention is simply intentional steps you can take, as a caregiver, to de-escalate behaviors before they grow to an aggressive, agitated, or violent level, or stop them from happening in the first place. *Intervention*, however, are strategies you can apply when your child is already at an escalated behavioral state, to quickly de-escalate the situation and help them re-regulate.

While behavior management has several components, two aspects are key. And they are very powerful once you understand them and apply them to your journey. The reason is threefold:

(1) Understanding prevention and intervention strategies brings calm and re-regulation to circumstances with your child, which could otherwise move into an uncontrollable state.

(2) Applying prevention and intervention strategies reinforces secure attachments by focusing first on connection through regulation and understanding before correction or discipline.

(3) Using prevention and intervention strategies changes your perspective on your child.

These are important to understand as you work toward regulation first before discipline.

Prevention Strategies

You can take steps either to stop or drastically reduce behaviors before they start. To prevent bad behaviors, let's look at five key steps to follow.

Key #1: Look at Your Own Behavior Management

Years ago, we found ourselves in an *eight-hour* tantrum with one of our children. It involved not only us, but one of our habilitation providers and some of our older children. But when I (Mike) look back at that day, I see that my tone and reaction caused him to escalate. Instead of stepping back, asking myself some crucial questions, and approaching him differently, I immediately tried to correct the behavior. I demanded that he apologize for the names he was calling Kristin and his hab provider. I demanded that he pick up everything he had destroyed in our house. I raised my voice when I noticed that our other kids were becoming afraid. I misunderstood what was really going on and missed an opportunity to help him re-regulate his emotions.

Our own regulation is crucial in helping our children find calm quickly. Our tone, reaction, timing, attitude, language, and body language often determine the speed of escalation with our children. As caregivers, we must first take a hard look at our own emotional regulation. We can often become the biggest triggers for our children. In order to help a dysregulated child find re-regulation quickly, it's crucial for us to manage *our own* actions and reactions.

Consider your home environment and all you have going on. We understand how easy it is to become triggered by your child's behavior. We are emotionally involved with our children on this journey. It's easy to allow our emotions to get the best of us. It's often a tension to manage, not a problem we can solve. (We'll talk more in chapter 12 about how we can self-regulate.) But if we want to prevent their bad behavior, we'll regulate our emotions.

Key #2: Identify the Trigger

One hot August many years ago, we took our then-family-of-six to the Indiana State Fair. The fair has been a tradition for our family since 2003. This particular year, a sibling group we were caring for through foster care were joining us. We visited different barns with animals, rode the rides, sampled the tasty treats, and soaked up the warm summer air. As we were leaving the fairgrounds toward the end of night, we passed a group of Indiana State police officers who were tending to an ill fair-goer. As we passed them, EMTs drove up on a stretcher golf cart with their emergency lights flashing. This set the little girl we were caring for into a full-blown meltdown. A few days later, we found out from her case manager that the night she was removed from her parents' care, police and EMTs had to be involved. This was a trigger for her.

As we discussed at length in the previous chapter, we must become detectives with our children's behaviors. What may seem to be an obvious trigger may not be. It may be bigger than "I don't like spaghetti! It's gross! And you always make it even though I don't like it! You're not my real mom anyway! *I hate you!*" As you work backwards, you may eventually discover that five years earlier, the last meal his first mom cooked for him was spaghetti. He may not be able to articulate the emotions he's feeling verbally; his body may be reacting to something like spaghetti in a way that he doesn't understand.

Recognize the warning signs. One important thing Sarah walked Ben and Lacy through was to identify and recognize warning signs when Fiona's behavior was escalating. For example, they identified that when she began to feel dysregulated, she would squeeze her fists tightly, causing her knuckles to become white. This would happen even if she wasn't yet angry or in a rage. She would also stand on her tiptoes repeatedly. Ben and Lacy recognized that when this happened, they needed to be proactive in prevention strategies.

What does this look like for your particular situation? Once you have figured out those clues, you need to *recognize the warning signs.* The more tuned in you are, the more likely you'll be to head off the behavior before it becomes a full-blown meltdown. We live in central Indiana where it is flat and windy and we deal with severe weather often. Years ago, before advanced weather-tracking technology, people sometimes had less than a minute to react to the threat of a tornado. With the advancement of technology, we now receive on average between three to fourteen minutes' warning. We see and hear the signs—swirling clouds in the distance, sirens roaring—and have time to get to safety.

With our children, when we know what we're looking for, we can react quickly and in advance. One of our children begins rubbing his eyes when he is feeling dysregulated. When he was younger, he would rub his eyes so hard we thought he might do damage. We've learned that when we see this, we immediately go on alert, ask crucial questions, such as, "How can I help you right now?" or "I see that you're starting to feel upset; what can I do to make you feel better?" or change up what we are doing.

Recognizing the warning signs gives you advance warning that we're heading for a potential meltdown. When looking for warning signs, pay attention to patterns, dates, times, environments, seasons, sights, smells, and sounds that are happening when meltdowns occur.

Refer often to your behavior log. We already discussed the importance of gathering information in a journal or behavior log. But don't just log it, study it, so that when a trigger comes, you're aware of the circumstances and can respond immediately. Knowledge is power, they say. And your log gives you that knowledge.

Key #3: Invite Your Child to Know Themselves

Our goal is for our children to care for themselves and meet their own needs one day. They will learn these skills in child-hood. We must invite them to know themselves and their story. To understand how their brain works and how their body stores experiences. To share their story, their needs, their successes, and their boundaries with others. To problem-solve for themselves so they can confidently work through emotional dysregulation no matter the circumstance. Inviting our children to manage their own behaviors builds confidence and self-sufficiency. For instance, with one of our children, in particular, who is nearing adulthood, we've begun to help him identify how he's feeling leading up to anxious, erratic, or impulsive behaviors. By helping him identify his feelings, and then listing things he can do to help regulate himself or cope with difficult situations, we are preparing him for life away from our direct care and guidance.

Key #4: Avoid the Triggers

This seems obvious, doesn't it? But when we get busy or dis-tracted or complacent, it can be easy to rush ahead with life and then find ourselves in the middle of a meltdown, wondering what happened. Our children need us to be ever vigilant.

Plan ahead. You might not be able to avoid all triggers. If you know that something difficult is coming, such as a trip to Walmart, which typically causes bad behavior, then plan ahead.

Talk with your child first. You may say, "We have to go to Walmart, and I know you have a hard time there. But Mommy's going to be right there with you the entire time. We are only going to spend [insert time frame] there, and then we're going to leave." Or ask, "What can we pack to help you feel calm when we're in Walmart?"

Know exactly what you have to get, what part of the store it's located in, and how much time it's going to take you to get there, get the item, check out, and get back to your car. Create an exit plan if things get too uncomfortable. You may need to leave your shopping cart at guest services and head to the car for a break. If you have to browse products, browse online first so you don't linger. Encourage your child to participate in the plan for success.

Be intentional. A few years ago when our son was struggling in one of his classes, we discovered that his teacher of record was out for an extended period and the school was filling her class with a rotating group of substitutes. The lack of consistency and structure caused our son to feel insecure and unsure every day he went to school. We made a plan with the school to create a more successful situation. Every morning on her way into her classroom, one of his teachers would stop by the library and check out a few books. When she noticed he was becoming restless, she would invite him to return the books to the library for her. It drastically reduced meltdowns throughout the day.

When you know what causes your child to become triggered easily, you can plan ahead with intentionality and purpose. If you know twinkling Christmas lights can be a trigger, be intentional about where you go during the holidays. If your child dislikes large crowds, choose a park, church, or shopping mall with fewer people.

Set attainable goals with your child and include your child in meeting those goals. "We are going to church this morning and we are going to stay for thirty minutes. I know you can do it. What are some things you would like to pack for the trip there?"

Get creative. Just as one of our son's teachers got creative with the library books, you may need to think outside the box to circumvent triggers and meltdowns. Get creative with your schedule and the structure you institute with your child. You may need to pull them out of school early to avoid the classroom holiday party and do something special as a family instead. You may need to pack special items, such as noise-cancelling headphones in order to make a trip to the zoo more enjoyable. Include your child in the creativity. Normally, we let our children decide what they want to take with them on outings such as to the zoo or to a park. Let them take ownership over the things that will help them be successful.

Key #5: Create a Backup Plan

The truth is, regardless of how well-planned-out you are, you may have to formulate a plan with your child in the event things become overwhelming or stressful. For example, every December we head to Ohio to visit family. We have such a large family, we have to make three different stops. Both sides of our family understand and accept that our family is different and that we have children who have special needs, react differently to affection, crowded noisy environments, or lots of activity. But even with extremely supportive extended families, our children may still need a change of pace. This is where a backup plan comes into play. This is simply an understanding you have with your children that if things become too overwhelming, they can alert you, and you will respond.

An exit plan may mean going home, taking five minutes to walk together, giving them a hug, or offering a special handshake that lets your child know they are supported. An exit plan is a time to reset, pause, connect, and start over. What does a backup plan include?

Communication. If you know a situation may be difficult for your child, communicate about the situation first. Talk with your child and the trusted adults who are involved. Make a plan for how you will exit the situation if necessary. Agree with your child that if something becomes overwhelming or too much, they can find you, and you will take a walk with them or move to a quiet room of the house.

A code word or sentence. A couple of years ago, we had nearly fifty people at our house for my (Mike's) fortieth birthday party. At the time, we lived in a small farmhouse, and anytime more than ten people gathered, the house felt cramped. It quickly became overwhelming to one of our children who struggles with lots of chaos and activity. As I interacted with guests, I felt the warmth of a tiny hand grab hold of mine. I looked down to see my little guy gazing up at me. I quickly noted the anxiety in his eyes. He squeezed my hand three times, which was our code for the feeling of anxiousness. I squeezed back and then ended my conversation with a guest. Then he and I took a walk into his bedroom and closed the door.

I looked at a book with him for a few minutes, hugged him, and asked if he would like to spend more time in his room. He nodded. Then I asked if he would like the door open or closed. He chose to have it closed so I told him how proud I was that he was regulating on his own. Then I closed the door and let him join the party again when he was ready.

A code word, phrase, or action can be something no one will understand except you and your child. No one will know what is going on if your child says, "Poodles," in the middle of the church lobby, but you and your child will know. It could be a phrase like, *Are we almost out of milk?* It might seem random to passersby at the town fall festival, but most people won't give it a second thought. You and your child will know what the phrase means. The code can be a gesture like winking or a hand squeeze. No one else will notice, and you and your child will know that something is causing feelings of discomfort.

You may say, "I notice sometimes being with a lot of people can feel overwhelming. I want to help you when we are in those situations. We could go for a walk, have a squeeze, or make an excuse to leave, but I need to know when you are reaching your limit. So let's create a word that will be our secret code that you can use when you feel like you're getting overwhelmed."

You can practice the scenario with your child. Let's say the code word is *pickles*. When the child says, "Pickles," stop what you are doing, make eye contact, and find out what they need. You may also want to come up with a response beforehand that lets your child know that you have heard them and you will be with them as soon as possible.

Intervention Strategies

Though we hope to prevent extreme behaviors, dysregulation, or anxiety with careful preparation, it simply isn't always possible. We may find our children can escalate or become triggered without much, if any, warning. When this happens, we must help our child re-regulate and return to a place of calm. This is where intervention strategies come into play.

Know your first goal. A few years ago, one of our children became extremely dysregulated quickly. He walked into the living room where the rest of our children were quietly playing a video game together. He asked if he could play, and no one answered. That was a trigger.

Why did the children say nothing? They had grown so accustomed to verbal and physical attacks from their brother that they were all frozen. They, too, were displaying a trauma response.

Over the next few minutes, the emotional temperature in the room rose. Soon, all the children were angry, scared, and fighting with each other. My instinct was to shut down the behavior and demand that the first child make it right with his brothers and sisters. Since this child was not able to function in the logical brain, my first goal was to help him calm down. I moved between my son and his siblings, spoke softly, and asked him if I could talk to him in the next room.

He followed me into the next room, all the while hurling insults back at his siblings. When we finally made it to the other room, I asked him what was going on with him. He thought about it for a moment, then blurted out, "I'm really tired and I want to go to bed!"

"Okay," I said. "How about I help you get into bed?" We walked together to his bedroom, and I waited for him to change into his pajamas and crawl into his bed. After thirty minutes or so, he was calm and nestled warmly beneath his covers.

After he'd re-regulated, Kristin walked into his room, stood next to his bed, and stated very calmly, "What you did a little while ago was really scary for your brothers and sisters. You need to apologize to them tomorrow. Okay?"

Our son nodded. And the next morning he went to each of his siblings and made amends.

Had Kristin stormed into the living room while the uproar was happening and demanded that our son make things right, apologize, and stop scaring the other children, his behavior would have only escalated. It was only in a regulated state (or the return to his prefrontal cortex) that he could comprehend her request and follow through.

Our first goal is not correction and it isn't discipline. Yet. Our first and *only* goal when our child has become dysregulated, agitated, triggered, anxious, or aggressive is re-regulation. (We will talk about strategies for regulation throughout the next few chapters.) This may be hard to grasp. Maybe you were raised in a traditional household as the two of us were. If we misbehaved, talked back, or were disrespectful, our parents disciplined us. I (Mike) distinctly remember moments when my parents cracked down on my behavior, corrected the path I was on, and I never repeated the behavior again. They could do this, though, because I was functioning from the logical part of my brain.

Remember that when the amygdala, or alarm system, in a person's brain flips, it overrides the prefrontal cortex where logic, reasoning, and self-control exist. Our children's alarm systems have triggered so many times that they have actually malfunctioned. This is why we cannot attempt to correct their behavior, or emphasize a consequence, in the middle of a meltdown.

We know that when we wrong someone, the right thing to do is to make it right, ask forgiveness, and achieve peace with the other person. The brain that is in survival mode cannot correct the behavior until it is calmly functioning and able to reason and use logic. That's why we must first help our dysregulated child re-regulate. Start by asking yourself, "How can I de-escalate this situation?"

Connect before any correction. We learned this concept from Dr. Karyn Purvis at an Empowered to Connect live event, and it has worked wonders in our home. Sometimes we just want to respond to our child's behavior with, "What's wrong with you?" or "Why are you acting like this?" We want the behavior to stop. But we must always connect first. With our children, we must learn to reverse our questions when their behavior has escalated.

Instead of, "What's wrong with you?" ask, "How can I help you?"

Instead of, "Why are you acting like this?" acknowledge their emotions and say, "I can see you're upset right now. What can I do to help you feel better?"

Instead of "Stop this" or "That's enough," tell them "It's okay to feel upset. I'm here to help you. How can I make you feel better?"

Asking "What's wrong with you?" builds a wall between you and your child, whereas asking "How can I help you?" builds a bridge.

Bring it full circle. You may be thinking, *This seems wrong! My child is flipping out, screaming at people, breaking things, and I'm supposed to help them calm down before I discipline or try to correct their behavior? That feels like I'm letting them off the hook!* We totally understand this feeling. Parenting with connection, focusing on re-regulation first, and functioning with a bigger picture in mind is a paradigm shift. It defies traditional parenting in every way because it targets a child's dysregulated state before it deals with behavior. We'll go one step further—it is an intense focus on the *reasoning behind* the behavior rather than the behavior itself.

You may also be wondering, *What about disrespect and the harm my child's behavior causes others? Are you saying we should excuse the damage because my child is acting out of survival brain?* Not at all. We need to teach our children respectful behavior, but we need to teach them only when their brain is ready and able to receive the correction. When we know our children are re-regulated emotionally, it's time to bring the incident full circle and guide them toward reconciliation. It's important for our children to hear us say, "The way you treated your sister today was hurtful." "Your teacher loves you, and the way you talked to her when we were leaving school was disrespectful." "I need to let you know that you hurt me when you screamed in my face. I know you feel upset.

When you feel better, I need you to make that right."

We need to bring this full circle for a couple reasons: (1) Our children have to learn how to function with others, even when they are feeling agitated or anxious; (2) we believe our children can and will be productive adults.

—————————— **What now?** ——————————

- Journal or discuss with a friend:
  - What are some behaviors that concern you?
  - What clues have you discovered about why those behaviors are happening?
  - What are specific steps you can take to prevent the situations that lead to those behaviors?

Remember . . .

- *Regulation is the first goal.*
- *You can prevent many unwanted behaviors by planning ahead.*
- *You decide what goals you set for your family.*

CHAPTER 11

MANAGING CRISIS BEHAVIOR

Four years after Steve and Melissa got married, they decided to start a family. However, they chose to adopt, rather than have children biologically, because, as they put it, "We decided that so many children needed a home, the right thing to do was to provide that forever home."

They signed up to become a foster-to-adopt family. Soon after, four-year-old Mary was placed in their care, followed a few months later by seven-year-old Marcus. Mary was compliant, calm, and sweet. Marcus was also loving, but very active and hard to control. Not only did he run to any person and hug them, whether he knew them or not, he also began acting out sexually while sitting on people's laps or being held in their arms. Soon he was diagnosed as having sexually maladaptive behavior. Steve and Melissa had to keep eyes on Marcus at all times, and eventually had to stop going out into public because of his behavior. They were in crisis. And they had no answers.

We've been working to get a handle on preventing or intervening when our children move into bad or disruptive behavior. But what happens when they exhibit behaviors that become harmful to self or others? This becomes what we call crisis behavior. The methods and strategies we looked at in earlier chapters won't work for these types of behaviors. We need to deal with them as we would with any crisis—immediately.

How We Know It's a Crisis Behavior

While we could safely consider lots of different behaviors crisis behaviors, let's look at some of the most prevalent that you may be dealing with in your home.

Sexual Acting Out

When Sadie's daughter was ten and her son was five, Sadie noticed something off between them. Her son no longer wanted to sit beside his sister on the couch, at the dinner table, or in the car.

At first Sadie brushed off the change. Then one night at bath time, her son referred to his penis as a googoo. Sadie corrected him right away and asked where he'd heard that term. He shrugged his shoulders and looked away. Though Sadie felt uncomfortable, she couldn't articulate the problem. The following week, the school counselor called to let her know that during the body-safety program in her son's kindergarten class, her son disclosed that his older sister often touched his private parts and asked him to keep it a secret.

Sadie wanted to deny the possibility that her daughter could be harming her son, but then she remembered the uncomfortable "gut" feeling she had been experiencing. She asked her mother to pick up her daughter after school that day, while Sadie picked up her son and took him immediately to a counselor. While the counselor and the department of child services interviewed her son, she waited in the lobby. The counselor concluded the story was true and contacted the police. Soon, a detective interrogated her daughter, who admitted she saw the sexual acts on an app on her tablet and acted them out on her brother. She said she knew it was wrong but did it anyway because she was curious.

That night, Sadie and her children had to meet with a social worker who created a safety plan that they were all to follow. The three of them signed the contract together.

For the next six months, they had an open case with the department of child services. Sadie agreed to sexually maladaptive therapy for her daughter and trauma-informed therapy for her son. Sadie joined a support group for parents as well. Their family will maintain the safety plan for the rest of their childhood. Eventually they will rebuild trust and the incident will not control them.

Violence

Grayson is often violent at home and school. He began the aggressive behavior at the age of two when he started clawing his foster mom's face, kicking her, and screaming. In elementary school, he broke toys, windows, and even his bedroom door off the hinges. As a middle schooler, his aggression turned toward his teachers and other students, and he was often suspended. When he became a high schooler, home became an increasingly unsafe place for his family. He became angry in an instant and would put his hands around his sister's throat, threaten to stab his mother, or break items in a fit of rage.

His family functioned from a constant place of hypervigilance. They had a safety plan, which included their other children hiding behind a locked door. Grayson's parents taught the other children to call 911 and follow a script they created if they needed police help: "Hello, this is Jackson. I live at [address]. My brother Grayson has a mental illness. He is [describe the behavior]. My brothers and sisters and I are in the upstairs bedroom with the door locked. My mom is downstairs talking to him. We need a crisis-intervention-trained officer. My brother is unarmed. All knives are locked up, and there are no weapons in the house."

When police arrived, Grayson usually calmed down and apologized. When he didn't calm, the police detained him and took him to the psychiatric unit at their local hospital. Grayson's mom usually followed the police car and waited the three to thirteen hours it took to get him admitted. For a few days he got stabilized at the hospital while the family got stabilized at home.

Though the children were well versed with the safety plan and their brother's mental illness, their constant feeling of unease took its toll on them. Eventually, after multiple stays in the psychiatric unit, the hospital social worker suggested that Grayson move to a residential facility. While Grayson's parents did not want him to experience the trauma of family separation, they knew they had to keep their other children safe. They also knew that they needed more support to keep him safe than what they could provide. While Grayson was an inpatient, his family sought counseling to help heal the trauma they had all experienced at his hands.

Harming Animals

Jed lived with his foster family on a farm since he was four years old. Jed was fun-loving and kind. But he struggled to stick up for himself at school and at home with his older siblings. Whenever things became stressful, he bottled his feelings inside. His parents noticed that the family dog and cat refused to go near Jed. They occasionally heard the dog yelp, but when they investigated, they couldn't find anything wrong. Even though Jed was nearby, he was watching television or reading a book and didn't seem to notice the animal.

One day they caught him pinching the dog. They confronted him. He denied hurting the animal but clenched his fists and retreated to his room.

"I saw what you did to the dog," Jed's dad said. "That's not okay. We don't ever harm animals."

Jed wouldn't look at his dad, so his dad asked to see his eyes. Jed looked up quickly, then looked away. "Thank you, Jed," his father said. Jed's dad became so frustrated with Jed's lack of response, though, that he stepped aside and allowed Jed's mom to take over.

"Jed, it is our job to look out for any living thing who is weaker than we are," she said.

Jed finally admitted, "I like the way it feels when they get hurt. I feel powerful."

Jed's parents stayed calm while they tried to figure out how to respond. Finally Jed's dad said, "I understand that you feel out of control sometimes. It can feel good to have power over someone else. But it is very scary to the dog. She feels afraid, just as you do."

Jed's parents made a quick safety plan before leaving the room. They told Jed that he was not to be in a room with an animal unless Mom and Dad were within eyesight. They told him they were all going to see a counselor to talk about how Jed was feeling and to work on ways to help him feel better and make better choices.

With the help of Jed's counselor, they were able to dig deeper into his feelings of loss and insecurity that prompted the behavior. They worked together as a family to help Jed keep himself and others safe. Over time, Jed found that by caring well for himself, he had less desire to harm others. Today he shows pigs for 4H and takes excellent care of them.

Verbal Assault

Becca was not physically aggressive, but her words did plenty of damage. She accused her foster parents of molesting her, a teacher of hitting her, and a peer of bullying her. The family and the school were investigated multiple times because of Becca's accusations. It became difficult to believe anything she said. At home Becca used her words as weapons with her siblings. She whispered to her sister that she was fat; she screamed at her brother that he was unwanted. Becca's family felt powerless to protect their other children and even themselves from Becca's words. Her parents decided that safety was their first priority and installed cameras in the home so they had proof of what was happening. They restricted Becca from being alone with other children. Sometimes this meant Becca had to go with them to the grocery store, Bible study, or even work.

Though Becca recognized her words hurt people, she did not have the impulse control to stop herself. She and her parents agreed to meet with a therapist to create strategies to gain control over her words. They also worked together to restore trust and relationship with the other members of the family and the school. Slowly she began to heal from her own bad feelings about herself. She found the strength to use uplifting words with others as well as make things right when she hurt someone verbally. Becca's siblings worked with their own therapists to create strategies to cope with Becca's verbal outbursts. With practice, they became skilled at walking away from her when she hurled insults. Becca wasn't able to be alone with her siblings until adulthood. As adults, the whole family is now able to have a relationship with one another that observes respectful boundaries with words.

Self-Harm

Jaden began self-harming when she was fourteen months old. When she was angry, bored, or sad, she would stick her finger in her eye or scratch herself until she bled. When she was a baby, her parents sewed the sleeves of her sleeper shut so she couldn't scratch herself. As she grew older, her self-harm behavior became more creative and dangerous. She cut herself with shards of glass, pencils, and the edges of furniture. Her parents had to keep their eyes on her constantly. They locked up anything sharp and checked her room each night.

With permission from the department of child services, they installed a camera in her room and a door alarm. They stayed in constant communication with her therapist and psychiatrist. Even though Jaden had an aide attend class with her, her self-harming behavior persisted. Jaden's parents made the difficult decision to admit her to the psychiatric unit of the hospital. They did not want her to feel further anxiety, but they realized they could not prevent her from harming herself. The hospital helped stabilize her medication so she could return home.

Now an adult, Jaden receives services through a federal program because of her disability. She is able to live in a group home and have a social worker, nurse, and habilitation provider who meet with her each week. She is doing well at her job and has learned to use her team for support when she feels like self-harming.

Running Away

George started running away when he was two years old. Whenever something didn't go his way, he took off. He ran toward traffic, jumped out of moving cars, and escaped from his school building. His parents often had to chase him through the store, neighborhood, and community. They knew George's running could cause him harm. They installed an alarm system on every door and alerted the police that George was a runner.

The police department in their community had a grant that provided tracking devices for children with disabilities who may be prone to disappearing. George is now a teenager, and the device finds him quickly when he runs. George works with his counselor, family, and teachers to learn ways to cope with his desire to escape. He works on a series of exercises each day, which his occupational therapist helped him create, and which help his body feel regulated. Thanks to his support system of his family and professionals, George is able to pursue safer ways to cope.

When Crisis Behavior Shows Itself

When our children show crisis behaviors, it can be scary and sad for us as caregivers. We may wonder how we missed the signs or if we could have done something to keep them from acting that way. Those wonderings do us no good, however. So how *do* we manage crisis behaviors? Here are eleven important steps:

Step 1: Don't Panic

When a child behaves in a harmful way toward self or others, our natural reaction is to make them stop immediately! When the child's behavior is shocking or unexpected, our reaction may be to panic. Here's the deal: If making them stop were a possibility, wouldn't we all just do that? When our children have big feelings, they aren't just acting out, they are reverting to their survival brain. Caregivers must shift the focus from stopping the behavior to helping the child return to a state of emotional regulation.

Caregivers must *self*-regulate first. You have to commit not to join them in that behavior. In other words, you cannot respond to a child who is throwing furniture by throwing more furniture. You need to get yourself to a place of calm. Take one deep breath, pause before responding, assess the situation, and then decide what to do. As people of faith, we use this moment to pray for God's leading. It might be something as simple as, "Lord, please help me see this child through Your eyes."

We set the temperature for what is happening with our children, so we must remain mindful of our facial expressions, our body language, and our tone. When we focus on regulating emotions first, we are not permitting the behavior, we are setting the environment for calm.

Step 2: Focus on Safety First

If a child is threatening suicide or homicide, we need to take these threats seriously. If a child has a weapon, we need to safely remove the weapon. A child may be throwing things, hitting, punching, kicking, or running into traffic. We try never to put hands on our children, but sometimes we must physically remove a weapon or stop a child from jumping out of a moving car or pull a child off another child they are harming.

If you feel you may need to physically restrain a child, you need to create a plan with a licensed therapist to learn therapeutic restraint and create a safety plan ahead of time so you know when and how to move a child to safety.

Step 3: Get Other Children to Safety

When you can't remove the aggressive child or the child is unable to re-regulate, you may need to get everyone else to safety until the child and the environment have returned to peace. Prepare a room or space ahead of time for them. Have a television, video games, books, or other activities, snacks, and a door that locks. Prepare your children with a code word so they will know when to go to this safe space, no questions.

If unsafe behavior is happening, we must also make sure our other children are able to cope with the trauma they are experiencing. Do your best to explain during a peaceful time what will happen if they need to get to a place of safety. Show them what they can do and try to make the space as peaceful as possible.

If the unsafe behavior is happening in a car, pull the car over and remove the child who is exhibiting unsafe behavior or remove the other children who are in harm's way. You may have to adjust your schedule or call on your support system so that children are not riding in the car together.

Step 4: De-Escalate the Situation

The way you respond to your child is key. You might say something like, "May I see your eyes? Thank you. I can see you're feeling dysregulated. I'm not mad. Does my face look angry?" We want to show our child that we aren't upset. Then hold your hands where the child can see them. "I am keeping my hands off of you. You don't need to feel ashamed. I'm not calling the police. You aren't grounded. I just want you to feel better. I'll wait while you get re-regulated."

This is not the time to correct. This is the time to de-escalate.

When we are thinking about disrespect, aggression, and defiance, it's hard to feel the empathy we need to help our child get re-regulated. If we allow the child who is melting down in the grocery store to change the trajectory of our shopping trip, it can seem as if they have won. Remember, this isn't a battle between you and your child, it is a battle you are entering *with* your child. Stopping to re-regulate during a shopping trip may mean the trip takes longer. It may mean that you compromise with your child and only do two stores instead of three. It may even mean that you stop for a snack in between errands.

Re-regulating will be well worth your time. A child who is re-regulated may be able to return to the task at hand with a renewed spirit. You may have spent an extra twenty minutes dealing with the dysregulation, but if you don't, you may end up facing the consequence of dysregulated feelings for the rest of the day. Re-regulation isn't spoiling. We re-regulate all day as adults, usually without thinking. We may be working and need to take a break to stretch our legs, use the bathroom, or fix a cup of coffee. Our children need to re-regulate but they don't yet have the skills to communicate their needs or meet those needs for themselves.

Step 5: Stay Calm and Firm

Who are you most likely to listen to? A calm and collected person who speaks with ease, has a focused demeanor, doesn't display heightened emotions? Or the person who is yelling, erratic, highly emotional, and speaks with harsh tones? We are more effective as caregivers when we maintain a calm and firm tone.

I (Mike) remember when we discovered how powerful *calm* and *firm* can be in our parenting toolbox. One Christmas, we had just returned home from seeing Christmas lights and shopping as a family. It was past bedtime, so we hurried to get all our children into bed. We were also both trying to tie up loose ends at work before powering down for the holidays. Everything seemed routine until one of our children melted down. He began to yell at us from his room, "I'm not going to bed!" His voice quickly became louder and his actions increasingly erratic. Amazingly, all of our other children were already asleep. Kristin checked to make sure their doors were shut, while I tried to reason with our child. He stood next to the dining room table with his arms folded while we sank into our chairs in exhaustion. Kristin and I turned to our laptops while our child threatened, screamed, and stomped his feet. Nothing we said or did helped.

Eventually he moved to our Christmas tree and began pulling ornaments off and throwing them across the room, shattering them against the wall behind us. Now I'll admit, as his behavior escalated, so did my temptation to lose my temper. I was tired, I was anxious to get work items wrapped up, and I was upset over this disrespectful behavior. As I could feel the emotions, and my own dysregulation, rising in me, I heard a ding on my computer. I looked down to see that Kristin had sent me a message: DON'T REACT TO THIS BEHAVIOR. DON'T SAY ANYTHING. IGNORE IT. STAY CALM. LET'S SEE WHAT HAPPENS.

Interesting, I thought. *Okay, I'll try this.* So I focused on my laptop and pretended to work. So did Kristin. The screaming and ornament breaking continued. A few times they were actually flying over our heads. It was extremely hard to ignore and not react. Kristin and I continued to text back and forth.

THERE'S NOTHING HE'S BREAKING THAT CANNOT BE REPLACED, Kristin's next text said. I cringed as I read this, thinking about some of the keepsakes on the tree, but she was right.

For the next ten minutes or so, our child raged and tried to engage us, and we said nothing. We were in the same room, so close in proximity, but completely disengaged verbally. We didn't even look up from our laptops. We decided this was not a hill to die on.

After several minutes of disengagement, out of the corner of my eye I saw my child's once-clenched fists slowly open. His hunched shoulders and arms relaxed. He quietly walked over and stood next to Kristin. "I'm sorry, Mom. I'll stop now."

She calmly looked at him and firmly said, "I accept your apology. Now I need you to clean up your mess." He walked into the kitchen and returned with the broom and dust pan. He cleaned up every broken piece of ornament in the dining room.

Choosing to stay close in proximity while keeping a calm tone can be a game changer.

Step 6: Create and Follow a Safety Plan

A safety plan is something a family agrees on to maintain safety in the home. In our home we follow multiple safety plans without even thinking about it. You do too. For instance, we wear our seat belts in the car every time we drive. It is unlikely that we will have an accident but if we do, we know the seat belt will help protect us from injury. In our homes we have smoke detectors and fire extinguishers. It isn't probable that our home will catch on fire, but if it does, we need to be prepared. A safety plan is a precaution. For crisis behaviors, a safety plan is a written plan that everyone in the family knows and understands. If the crisis behavior has come to the attention of law enforcement, department of child services, or the school, they may be involved in the safety planning as well. A safety plan should use simple, direct language.

Here is an example of a safety plan for a child who is fascinated with fire.

FIRE SAFETY PLAN
- We can have a fire with adult permission and supervision.
- We can have a fire in the fire pit.
- We can burn items that an adult has given permission to burn.

If a child takes a lighter into his room and tries to light paper on fire, he is not following the safety plan. If a child is enjoying a campfire with Mom and Dad but impulsively throws his Legos in the fire to see if they burn, he is not following the safety plan.

You can modify a safety plan to any situation. For instance, a safety plan for sexual acting out may look like:

SAFETY PLAN
- Each person has his or her own blanket on the couch.
- We use the bathroom, change our clothes, and bathe in private.
- One person in the bathroom at a time.
- We play where Mom and Dad can see us.
- We do not play behind closed doors.
- Private parts (lips, nipples, vagina, penis, and bottoms) are private. We do not touch anyone else's private parts or allow anyone else to touch ours.
- If we are curious about private parts, we can look at our own private parts in the bathroom.

• If we have any questions about sex or private parts, or if we need to talk about past sexual abuse, we can talk to our safe people (Mom, Dad, therapist).

A safety plan should be clear, simple to understand, and easy to follow. A safety plan is not for everyone else to know. If the child is exhibiting a crisis behavior at school, the teacher, guidance counselor, and resource teacher may need to know, but the cafeteria staff do not. A safety plan should protect your child, other children, and also maintain your child's dignity.

We do not attach consequences to safety plans because a child who is acting out of survival brain will do so without the ability to think logically. A child in survival brain is not able to connect a consequence with an action. A safety plan for dangerous behavior is the same as a safety plan for wearing a seat belt. We must wear a seat belt no matter what because it keeps us safe. If our child isn't able to follow the safety plan, it is our job as adults to modify the safety plan to include greater adult supervision.

Step 7: Respond with the Least Amount of Correction and Intervention Needed

It can be tricky to find an appropriate consequence when a child has acted out in a disrespectful, destructive, or dangerous way. We may want to react in a big way, hoping to get a big response. Unfortunately, that usually only ends up dysregulating both caregiver and child again, which will start the cycle over again.

Karyn Purvis and David Cross give us a wonderful outline for four levels of correction:[1]

Level One: Playful Engagement. A low-level challenge or mild disobedience—for example, mouthiness or verbal disrespect—may be met with playful engagement. If a child says a disrespectful word, we might respond with, "Uh-oh, let's try another word. I know how creative you are!"

Level Two: Structured Engagement. With a slightly elevated challenge, or moderate disobedience—such as when the child doesn't respond appropriately to playful engagement—the caregiver may offer choices. For instance, if the child refuses to clean up after dinner, you might say: "We all clean up after dinner. You may choose to clear your plate now and join us in the family room or you may choose to sit here until you are ready to clean up." You may anticipate that your child will choose neither, so control what you can control. You may say to the whole family, "Wow, that was a good dinner. I'm going to fix bowls of ice cream for dessert. Let me know when your chore is done; I'll check it, and then I'll scoop some ice cream for you." You may pause a minute and then say to everyone, or no one in particular, "I think I'm going to have chocolate; what's your favorite flavor?" You are giving a choice, controlling what you can control, and using distraction as a tactic.

Level Three: Calming Engagement. When your child nears full escalation or verbal aggression, we must be carefully attuned. At this level, we can give the child a chance to do "time-in" and think about what they need while the adult is nearby. We need to redirect verbal aggression first; then they can have time to think it over and get a chance to repair. A child who has verbally disrespectful behavior at dinnertime does not require a month long consequence. He will need to take steps to repair the relationship with the other family members and may need to spend time allowing the rest of the family to have peace. He may serve a consequence of no television after dinner or an earlier bedtime. He could start rebuilding the relationships with others by doing the after-dinner chores with Mom and Dad and giving siblings a break or volunteering to do an extra chore. If he is regulated enough after the outburst, he may be able to come up with a consequence for himself and serve it peacefully.

Level Four: Protective Engagement. This level shows significant threat of violence or harm by the child, either to himself or to someone else. You'll need to redirect the physical aggression first through verbal distraction and then redirect through physical interruption only if necessary. You may say, "Son, do not put your hands on others in this family. I'm going to send your brothers and sisters to watch television until you are safe. Would you like to take a walk or sit with me for a minute?" Your child may accept the distraction or choose neither. If the child is harming someone else, you may need to physically step in to protect the other child.

Step 8: Allow Natural Consequences

Many years ago, a child we cared for through foster care found herself arrested and charged with theft. She was guilty. In fact, she was caught on camera doing the act. There was nothing we could do or say to keep her from facing consequences. If your child is going to make poor choices, or do the opposite of what you tell them to do, you can only do so much. You cannot prevent that from happening; you can only guide them and remind them of the consequence if they choose that action. If they disregard coping mechanisms you've helped them learn, and physically attack someone, they will suffer repercussions. These are natural consequences, and we must allow them to play out.

All of our choices and behavior, good or bad, have repercussions. If we choose a life of love and peace, contentment will follow. If we choose a life of anger or discord, distrust and stress will follow. It's that simple.

Older children may face a consequence in the community or at school. If this is the case, support your child, advocate for your child, but do not rescue them. Sometimes the consequence your child received at school is enough. Your job is to empathize and help your child come up with a plan to do differently in the future. Sometimes a child may face a legal consequence, sit beside them in court, go with them to talk to police. Help them advocate for themselves as well.

Teach them to ask for a lawyer and not to talk without a parent or lawyer present. Sympathize when they have community service or visits with a probation officer. You are not shaming or creating a greater consequence; you are in a role of support. You may say something like "Yeah, I know this stinks. It's a bummer to have to pick up trash on a rainy cold day like this. I'm so glad you've learned your lesson." (Even if you aren't sure, give them the benefit of the doubt.) "Tonight when you get home, it's going to feel nice to get into a warm shower."

If our child ends up incarcerated for a crime they committed, we cannot protect them from facing this consequence. We cannot stop the police from arresting them, or a prosecutor from prosecuting them. We can become their number-one supporter. We attend every hearing, pray for them, visit them in prison, and continually encourage them.

Step 9: Control What You Can Control

Our default as parents is to try and control situations. If our child refuses to leave for school, we attempt to physically make them head out of the house to catch the bus. If our child refuses to turn off the Xbox or television when we tell him to, we attempt to gain control by taking the remote out of his hands.

If this is you, you've probably discovered it's a futile battle. So where does this leave us? We can only control what *we* can control with our children. We must ask ourselves in the midst of rising behaviors or battles for control, "What can I control here?"

Step 10: Document

If your child has behaviors that are dangerous to themselves and others, you will need to document the behaviors as well as the things you have put into place to help. Keeping a record will help you weed out which things are working and which are not. Keeping a record will also help you to protect yourself in the event of an investigation. Documenting can be in a spiral notebook with dates written at the top of the page or over email. You should include those in your support system in the documentation. This can be your child's caseworker, teacher, therapist, habilitation provider, attorney, or doctor.

Step 11: Call for Support

In our own home, we have a safety plan that includes calling for help when needed. When our child isn't able to keep themselves or others safe, we may need someone to watch our other children or we may need a crisis-intervention-trained officer to help us get them to the hospital. We may just need a trusted adult to talk with our child for a bit while they calm down.

When your child is having a crisis behavior, you need to call for support. Do not stay in isolation. Your support system may consist of only a few people and that's okay. They need to be people who listen without judgment, help your child and your family get to safety, and who will still care for your child when the crisis is over. This needs to be a person who understands your safety plan and who can offer tangible support.

When Law Enforcement Gets Involved

A child who is caught stealing, starting fires, vandalizing, sneaking out, fighting, or needs help getting to a psychiatric hospital may come face-to-face with law enforcement. The caregiver may need to call the police if their child is hurting themselves or someone else. If you find yourself involved with police, make sure to state clearly any diagnosis your child has. Explain to dispatch that your child has experienced significant childhood trauma and they are not able to regulate or reason. Ask for a crisis-intervention-trained officer. Though your police department may not have one available, you need to ask anyway. Alert them to anything they can expect from your child. If your child will yell, run, or fight, the police need to know this information. If they have a weapon, the police need to know. If they do not have access to a weapon, the police also need to know. If they have something that looks like a weapon, even something as benign as a pencil or a matchbox car, let the dispatcher know this as well. Give them any advice they may need to communicate with the child. You may ask for them to arrive without lights or sirens. You may encourage them to use the child's nickname instead of their full name.

If your child is arrested when you are not present, make sure they have a lawyer present before talking to police. Practice at home asking for a court-appointed attorney. We know this sounds like a bit much. Unfortunately, they may need this skill. If your child has impulsive behaviors, self-harming behaviors, or aggressive tendencies, they may find themselves in trouble and they need to know what to do to advocate for themselves. The court-appointed attorney is usually more familiar with that particular court and the judge your child will face. Your child needs to be able to ask for this representation if they get in trouble and you aren't there.

When your child begins driving, they need to practice what to do if they get pulled over. They need to have all of their documentation ready and easily accessible. In some states, a person with a disability can apply for a driver's license that has a code that alerts the police to a diagnosis, mental illness, verbal delay, etc., that may make communication difficult.

Interacting with law enforcement needs to happen long before a crisis situation. You can meet your local police at a community event or you can set up a time to talk with local law enforcement privately. Make sure your child knows them and that they know your child. They will be more likely to help resolve a crisis when they know your child personally.

Teaching Reconciliation and Restoration

It is tempting to lecture right in the middle of the behavior or immediately after. Forgive yourself if you start to do this. Once you are both at peace, return to the incident. This may be an hour later or the next day. It can feel wrong to allow time to go by but remember that if you are still talking to your child's survival brain, you won't make any progress anyway. Conserve your energy and have the conversation later. Tell your child, "This behavior made me feel . . ." Ask your child, "How were you feeling? What was going on inside your body? What was happening around you?" Then listen! Don't talk. Hear them out, even if you disagree or observed something else. Then ask, "What can we do next time?"

When a child's behavior has resulted in damage to items or relationships, the child will need to make repairs. If a child punches a hole in the wall, they should participate in the repair. If a child hurts someone's feelings, they should write a note of apology. If a child steals something, they should return the item, apologize, and take the consequences.

Some children may need external help throughout their lifetimes. That's okay. Whenever they are able to take any type of self-control and responsibility, we can celebrate.

What Now?

- Journal or discuss with a friend:
  - What kind of safety plan can you create with the help of your child? Who are safe people who can support when things are difficult?

Remember . . .

- *Safety first.*
- *You set the tone. Calm and firm win the day.*
- *Correction happens in a place of logical thinking.*

CHAPTER 12

EMOTIONAL REGULATION AND SELF-CARE FOR THE CAREGIVER

If we intend to help our children regulate, we must first be able to regulate ourselves. Often Mike and I are asked, "How do you stay so calm?" The truth is, we don't. We react to stress just as any other human does. Our bodies and minds have stored all of our own past trauma experiences and combined them with our personalities, which are written into our DNA. For me (Kristin), my natural response to most stress is to cry. My natural response to happiness is to cry. My natural response to anger is to cry. You may be seeing a pattern here. It isn't reasonable to expect me to just stop crying. My body wants to cry—I can't help it.

Another of my responses is to fight. If I see something wrong, I want to fight for justice. I want to fight if I see danger. I will often run toward a problem before stopping to consider all the implications. This is my body's natural response. To expect that I will bypass this response in an emergency situation is unreasonable. However, to allow myself to respond to each and every stressful situation by fighting isn't a reasonable expectation either.

If I'm driving on an icy road and my car suddenly skids into a retention pond next to a neighborhood, my trauma response to fight my way out of the sinking car just might save my life and my family's lives. However, if I am having a disagreement with another mom at playgroup over the toy her kid just took from mine, it would be inappropriate for me to claw the toy out of the toddler's tiny grip. Before I can ever help my child regulate, I must first be able to lead by example. My body is wired to handle stress in a certain way. My own experiences have left me with memories that will color my perspective on things I experience in the future. Because I know these things about myself, I can manage my body's natural responses and I can set myself up for success when facing most uncomfortable situations. By self-regulating, I am setting an example for my children to follow when they face their own triggers.

The same is true for you. If we don't know how to manage ourselves well, we can't help our children manage their own emotions and needs well. But when we do manage ourselves well, we can offer our children great models for how they can be better.

Pay Attention to Who You Are and How You React

We can't know and understand another person until we first know and understand ourselves. That means first we must identify what our regulated body looks and feels like. When we are regulated, we feel at peace, we are productive, and we are focused. When we are at peace, we have a general sense of well-being. We might smile. Our hands may rest relaxed at our sides. Our breathing steadily fills our lungs. How do you feel when you are regulated?

Then we need to identify what our body looks and feels like

when we are exiting our regulated state. As I mentioned above, I can become weepy or ready to fight. Pay attention to your body and emotions when you become dysregulated. Your hands may clench; your breathing may become irregular. You may feel tingling or restlessness in your limbs. You may shake. Your body temperature may rise. Maybe your tone becomes high pitched or low and quiet. You may feel spaced out or jumpy. You may feel as though you can't focus. You may feel anxious or angry. You may feel the stress of dysregulation in your fingertips or as a ringing in your ears. You may have a tendency to yell or to retreat. You may hide and disengage or become hypervigilant trying to control the world around you. Just as you need to observe your children to help them, so you must observe your own regulation and dysregulation issues.

Know Your Triggers

Our five senses exist to give our bodies a clue about what is going on in the world around us. We can feel the temperature and adjust accordingly without much thought. We can smell fresh-baked cookies causing our tummy to rumble or the spray of a skunk causing us to wrinkle our nose and warning us to get away. Our bodies and brains also store the information collected by our five senses. When we smell fresh-baked cookies, our brain pulls up a memory. We recognize the smell and we know what to expect. We may also remember with vivid accuracy a time when our next-door neighbor shared a plate of cookies with us on a snowy day. Without much thought, we begin to smile. The smell triggered the memory; the memory triggered a response.

The same things happen with memories that are attached to trauma. If we grew up in a home surrounded by fighting, raised voices may be a trigger for us. If an older sibling embarrassed us, we may be triggered by a strained relationship between our children.

If we were never affirmed by our parents, we may be triggered by a child who screams, "You are the worst mom ever!"

Think about your triggers. Knowing them helps you prepare when your reactions to your children are less than ideal. Thinking ahead helps you to be ready so you can react to your children from an emotionally regulated state of mind.

Understand Your Own Experience with Trauma

I (Mike) have already recounted several traumatic experiences I went through as a child. And I have spent time understanding my personal experience with trauma and how it's affected me as an adult. For instance, I don't like it when people are hurting or made to feel stupid. Two of my daughters are currently seniors. Because of the COVID-19 pandemic, one of their activities recently cancelled was "senior pranks." As they lamented the loss of this cherished activity, all I could think was, *Good! I would hate for anyone to feel stupid, or embarrassed, or on display.* As I processed this, I traced it back to my junior high days when I was routinely made fun of and picked on. That experience has changed how I see the world, and how I feel about people being made to feel less than or on display (in a bad way). As you thought about your own experiences with trauma, your body responded as well. You may have pictured what your home looked like after being ravaged by a tornado, or the feeling of standing beside your beloved auntie's grave. These memories stirred an emotional reaction that your body kept stored inside.

When we know where we've been and recognize the toll those experiences have taken on us, we can anticipate what triggers may come in our everyday lives that bring up those emotional reactions. When we anticipate what may happen, such as someone being made fun of or made to feel stupid, we can prepare our bodies to respond in a regulated way. Sometimes we can't stop ourselves from reacting and that's okay. We may cry every time we hear "Amazing Grace," but we don't continue to cry twenty-four hours a day for the rest of our lives just because we heard that song. Instead, we react and then we return ourselves to an emotionally regulated state. Knowing our own trauma helps us to understand ourselves. Understanding ourselves will lead to empathy for our children's experiences with trauma and their reactions to their own triggers.

Self-Regulating after Our Children Trigger Us

I (Mike) am going to be honest here. There are days where I think about getting in my car and driving right down to a local pub, and drowning my sorrows and exhaustion. However, I don't. I believe pain and exhaustion are part of the human experience,[1] and thus, I keep traveling. As a person of faith, I also believe my Creator steps into those messy moments with me. Sometimes just a desperate prayer such as "Jesus, help!" is all I can squeak out.

So what do we do when we are trying to help our child re-regulate but we've become triggered? There are a few things we can do to get ourselves back to a regulated state.

Walk Away

Use this strategy if you can. We can't walk away from a two-year-old, but we can walk away from a fifteen-year-old. It's okay to say, "I'm going to need to step away for a minute," or "I'm going to use the bathroom, I'll be right back." With our younger children or with a child who cannot understand our perspective, Mike and I will usually make an excuse like we need to get a drink of water or we have to let the dog out.

As our children grow in maturity, we can let them know exactly what we're doing. For instance, we can say, "Your behavior is making me feel uncomfortable. I am going to walk away for a few minutes and get myself regulated."

Take Five Minutes before Answering

I (Kristin) often feel like the role of parent should automatically mean that I have all the answers. This simply isn't true. I don't always know what to do in the moment. Sometimes I need a break and a little perspective. When dealing with a dysregulated toddler, I have to remind myself that it is okay to close my mouth and not respond for five minutes. With an older child, the arguments, pushback, and emotions get much more complicated. When we are dealing with a teenager who is dysregulated, a simple conversation about curfew can lead to a rabbit trail about college exams, grades, boyfriends, adoption insecurities, and past relational hurts. Stop.

When you feel you are joining your child in their dysregulation, just stop. If the original conversation was about homework, return to that subject. Say, "I am happy to discuss curfew. I need five minutes to think it over, and I'll get back to you." During these five minutes, do not discuss anything else. Call your spouse or a trusted friend to talk logically over the situation. Get out a piece of paper and make a list of what you need to communicate, narrow that list down, and return to your child ready to discuss the decision you have made. This still opens you up to listen to what your child has to say and how they are feeling, but it resets your own brain to be able to focus on where you stand and understand yourself clearly.

Count

When you have a child who is stuck in a state of dysregulation, you can become tempted to try to talk them out of it or even physically remove them from their feelings of frustration. This won't work. So count in your head.

You may have a child who completely freezes when upset. Try to allow that child to return to their logical brain. If you're like me (Kristin), you want to talk her through it. Don't. Count in your head. Give the request or question and then pause and count to one hundred before saying a word. Then repeat the request or question simply and count again.

If you have a child who rages or yells insults, do not join them. Simply make your request or ask your question and then mentally count to one hundred before asking again. Do not engage in their emotional wandering. Stick to the issue that needs to be addressed. Keep language simple, then count. While you are counting, focus on regulating your heartbeat and breath.

Breathe

We breathe without any thought, but our breath is often a good indication of our state of emotional regulation. When our children are dysregulated, we react emotionally as well. Our heart rate quickens and our breathing becomes ragged as our bodies respond to our environment. We can focus on our breathing and returning to calm even in the midst of a crisis. One way we can do this is by Four Square Breathing. This concept comes from Dialectic Behavioral Therapy, or DBT.[2] Four Square Breathing is breathing in for four counts, holding for four counts, breathing out for four counts, holding for four counts, and repeating four times. Just by paying attention to our breathing, we can begin to regulate the rest of our body.

Give Your Ears a Break

Sometimes our children try to control their environment by their words or their tone. Understanding that this need for control comes from a feeling of insecurity can help us to respond with understanding and patience. That is our job; however, it is only natural that we will have an emotional response to our child's words and actions.

If your child verbally assaults you when they are feeling upset, put on headphones and listen to a song or an audiobook. Let them return to their logical brain before reengaging with them. Caring for yourself in the midst of caring for your child is a must. If you allow your ears to take a break, you will be better able to hear what your child is truly trying to communicate later.

Focus on Funny

Carry a funny book with you or listen to a humorous podcast. Send your friend a humorous text or log onto a comedy website. Laughter really is the best medicine. It's okay to laugh in the midst of stressful times. Laughter can be a wonderful reset to your own brain. If you and your child share a sense of humor, invite them to hear or see something funny too. I (Kristin) can't tell you how many times I have been at my wits' end with a child who all of a sudden turned the table on me and told me a joke. It's okay to laugh. Later you will return to the conversation or experience that caused the dysregulation in the first place. You and your child may need to repair damaged feelings, but first have a good laugh.

Connect to Your Tribe

Connection is so important for adults too. Both Kristin and I have contacts in our phones saved under "Favorites." These are people we can reach out to when we need perspective, encouragement, or prayer. This is our tribe, our inner circle, our most trusted allies. I (Mike) have four close friends I vent to, rant with, celebrate with, and hurt with. When things are not going well with our children, or I need to take a moment to connect with a neutral party to get a clear perspective, I retreat to my back porch and reach out to my tribe. When I'm chatting on the phone with them, it's as though we're standing next to each other.

When we talk and share, the guiding rules are as follows: *Listen without interruption. No fixing. Walk away loved.* We have a pact with one another. When one of us is in need, the rest of us commit to listening to their heart, perspective, and brokenness without interruption. We also commit ourselves not to offer fix-it solutions. Finally, we always leave with love for one another. Connection to people who understand you and your family is vital.

Say Something Positive

Words have power. Say something positive out loud to yourself and to your child. In the midst of a moment of dysregulation, I (Kristin) might say something like, "I am proud of myself for making dinner even though I hate cooking!" or I might say to my child, "I am happy that you cleaned your room today. It looks amazing and I'm really proud of you!" Either statement might catch our child off guard. It may serve as an interrupter to the train of thought they are on. It may do nothing. It may just help change my own mood. The only thing it will not do is cause harm.

Saying something positive is always a mood booster and a regulator. We all want to hear something good about ourselves, even when it comes out of our own mouths. As a side note: you can also write these words of affirmation and refer back to them. Write something positive on a sticky note and put it on the bathroom mirror or the coffee maker. Intentionally remind yourself and your child that you both are doing a good job.

Overall Self-Regulation and Self-Care Strategies

A crucial step in our self-regulation is self-care. Over our nearly two decades of parenting, we have learned something important: you cannot adequately care for your children, or your family, if you are not adequately caring for yourself. But I'll (Mike) go one step beyond this: you put your children and your family at risk when you're not adequately caring for yourself. There's no better illustration than that of an airplane. Board any flight and, as the aircraft taxies toward the runway, you will hear the flight attendant say,

"In the event that we lose cabin pressure, oxygen masks will automatically deploy from above you. If you are traveling with young children, we ask you to first secure your mask, before securing your child's mask." Why do they tell you this? It's simple. If you haven't taken the time necessary to make sure you are taken care of, and you pass out from the change in pressure, you are putting both your and your child's life at risk. What, then, does self-care look like for foster and adoptive parents?

Take a Break

We live on a farm in the middle of nowhere. In order for me to refresh my mind, I often take a walk to our barn to collect eggs, to our mailbox to collect the mail, or even just walk ten minutes around our property. Doing this helps my mind refresh itself and reset to the task at hand. Plus, it fills me spiritually, mentally, and emotionally.

Take five minutes for a walk. Take a night out or even a weekend away. You need a break. You are raising a child who is reacting out of trauma, and that is a big responsibility. Give yourself a few minutes a day that are just for you. You can do this even if you have to take the time immediately when the child falls asleep or right before they walk in the door from school. Allow some time that isn't about this very important job that you are doing.

Prepare Ahead of time

Several years ago, when one of our older children was in middle school, we routinely dealt with meltdowns right after he stepped off the bus and into our house. He had the ability to keep it together all day long, but then he lost it the second he stepped through our door. He felt safe enough at home to let down the walls, but not in other environments with other people. I (Mike) was often frustrated and exhausted soon after his arrival. I wondered how he could keep it together at school, but terrorize everyone in the family when he was home. This led to my own dysregulation, which did nothing to help him re-regulate. I found myself on edge, anxious, and rushed, trying to pull it together and change gears as he trotted off the bus. It was the equivalent of driving down the road and suddenly shifting the car in reverse. It would not be good for the transmission of a car, and trying to shift into a responsive mode to my child's dysregulated behavior was not good for my mental or emotional well-being.

During one of our counseling appointments, the therapist pointed this out and encouraged me to mentally rehearse his homecoming before he arrived. It worked. An hour before the bus pulled up, I began preparing myself. I made sure we were functioning tightly within our structure. I followed our laid-out routine. The snack was out and ready. The schedule was written down on a small whiteboard hanging in the kitchen. I mentally reminded myself that a child had just spent an entire day holding back his emotions. Simply walking myself through these mental exercises helped me remain in the right frame of mind and respond in peace and calmness.

I noticed something in my own state of mind soon after making this shift. When I was regulated, my child was quicker to return to regulation. When I was calm, he was able to move from anxious to calm more easily. When I was at peace, and kept my tone peaceful, he was more likely to be at peace.

When we can identify triggers—both theirs and ours—we can prepare to avoid them altogether or face them with a strategy in place.

Find Something You and Your Child Have in Common

We are creatures of connection. We crave relational connections with those around us. When we are raising children who lack the ability to reciprocate that connection, we can feel exhausted. No amount of knowledge about our child's brain, response, or reactions can cause us not to care about the connectedness we desire to feel with them. So find something you and your child have in common. It might be a funny cartoon, a favorite book, a sports figure, a type of food or song. Whenever you connect with your child over this, you will feel filled, too, even if only for a few moments. This feeling of connectedness can get you through the times when you find yourself feeling very disconnected. I (Mike) love to make up silly, spur-of-the-moment games to play. So do my three youngest sons. We will often play for hours on our trampoline in the backyard making up fun challenge games together. I've noticed often that even when I feel like the day is wasted, or that I'm not connecting with my children, some time together on the trampoline laughing and bouncing helps remedy this.

Take Care of Yourself

Years ago, we found ourselves in a desperate and lonely place. We'd received an official diagnosis of alcohol-related neurodevelopmental disorder (ARND) for our son, who at the time was almost six. This diagnosis falls under the umbrella of fetal alcohol spectrum disorders (FASDs). It brought us closure to finally have an official diagnosis and allowed us to move forward with some sort of plan. It also meant that he would never grow out of his difficulties. We were constantly vigilant. We had to have our eyes on him at all times and we couldn't allow him to be alone with his siblings, ever. We couldn't take long car rides or have any unstructured days. We had to plan every moment with him and strictly keep to a routine. No one could babysit him or provide respite. It was exhausting to the zillionth degree.

We were emotionally, physically, and spiritually spent. For two years, we hunkered down in our house, with shades drawn, lights off, shutting out the world. While we knew isolation wasn't healthy, we convinced ourselves that it was easier this way, and it sure did feel safer at the time.

We were totally isolated and we didn't see any way out of this circumstance. Our intimacy as a couple suffered, as well as our individual emotional health. But our journey back to hope began in May 2011 when a good friend invited us to a support group for post-adoptive families. Our first response was resistance. We were afraid to expose ourselves to the judgment of others. We were afraid that the meeting would reveal that we were, as we had begun to suspect, to blame.

Our friend told us that they would have free food and free childcare. That was the ticket. We signed up right away. It was the closest thing to a date night we'd had in a long time. A week later, we made our way to downtown Indianapolis. While we thought our child was the only one who acted out aggressively, and we were the only parents in the world who felt this way and lived in isolation, we discovered we weren't actually alone. There were others. We walked away from that first meeting feeling hopeful for the first time in many years. We felt connected and encouraged to change the way we cared for our family and ourselves. We discovered the great importance of self-care for us. We'd spent so many years pouring everything into our children (and rightfully so) that we had completely neglected the care of us.

We outlined some critical things we needed to change, such as the reinstitution of date nights and reserved time in the evenings, after kids were in bed, to be together as a couple, and we put them into practice. It changed everything for us.

Parenting children with trauma histories is really hard at times! This can take the life out of us and make us feel hopeless. We know we can't just stop parenting in order to care for ourselves, but we must find a balance. It begins when we change our perspective on self-care.

How do we make sure we are taking care of ourselves so we can take care of our children? Here are some keys we have learned to do personally. And they work!

Call out for help. When I (Mike) was in fourth grade, I was failing math. I wouldn't raise my hand for fear of feeling stupid. Not raising my hand didn't change my circumstances. I may have felt safer, but I was still failing. Sometimes we need help. As people of faith, prayer is one way we have called out for help. And trust us, sometimes, it's nothing more than a desperate "Jesus, help us!" call.

Take a time-out. The purpose of a time-out is to reset. Often we can't use time out with children who have experienced trauma, but we can use it on ourselves. We can use a time-out to reflect on how we got off course and what we can do to fix it. When we talk about taking time for you, we're not necessarily talking about a weekend getaway to the mountains or a beach. Taking a time-out is about taking time for you to think, breathe, pray, or just be. For example, one or two days a week, right after you get your children off to school, take an hour to go on a walk, exercise, read a book, or take a nap. If you work outside the home, use your commute to work as your "time-out." Or leave a bit earlier and stop by your favorite coffee shop. Turn your phone and email off during lunch and head to a park for solitude. If you're a stay-at-home parent, instead of stressing every day over laundry, take one day and choose not to fold another basket for an hour so you can rest. Intentionally plan time once a month for a night out with friends or attend a Bible study group. There are so many ways you can take time for you. You must be intentional—it won't happen by chance.

Find and engage in community. We can't do this alone. We need to surround ourselves with other foster and adoptive parents. We need four types of supportive people.[3]

First, we need people who limp like we do. Simply discovering that other people limp the way we do can be healing and cathartic.

Second, we need people who get it. In other words, get this. These people won't blink or flinch even if you share the hardest or most embarrassing story imaginable with them. They are also people who love you and your children regardless of your situation or the struggles your child has.

Third, we need people who are nonjudgmental. I don't need someone to make me feel more like a failure as a parent than I already do. This goes without saying, but you and I need to avoid judgmental people at all costs.

Fourth, we need people who have the emotional, mental, and spiritual health to point us in a direction that leads to our own growth and improved health. These are people who will listen to us without judgment, be there when we need to dump our emotional trucks on them, but then point us in a better direction of thought and action.

This is the very reason we started a virtual support and resource site exclusively for foster and adoptive parents called Oasis Community. We know how much we need this support, and we know how much you need this support. You can try it out for free for fourteen days here: www.oasiscommunity.me. We were never meant to journey along on our own.

Recalibrate your course. Sometimes the course you're on with your children isn't working. And you know it pretty quickly, right? When this happens, it's important to hit the reset button.

Back in 2015, I (Mike) was in the mountains of Tennessee speaking at a conference. Because I travel a lot, I try to stay in shape by exercising whenever I can. At this particular location, I was on a beautiful small college campus with lots of paths to run on. I woke up the first morning and went for a three-mile jog. I set my course and activated the running app on my phone. The next morning, I took the same route. But after I took off running, I immediately knew something was wrong with the app. The voice on the app that told me how much distance I had run suddenly told me I'd completed my run. I wasn't even near the halfway point.

After reading a review on the app, I discovered that I had to recalibrate the app with the satellite by following a few simple steps. After I did that, the app was back to normal, and I enjoyed great runs the rest of the week. That wouldn't have happened had I not stopped and taken the time to hit the reset button. This is the same thing we need to do when we realize we have gotten off course in our parenting, in our health, and in our care of ourselves. You may need to stop what you're doing and reach out to someone who can help you get back on course. Maybe you need to schedule a doctor appointment, call a friend, drink more water, or make sure you get more sleep. Whatever it is, it's time to recalibrate your course.

Order your days. One of the biggest enemies of self-care is a lack of structure. We are busy people, and we are parenting children who need a lot of our attention and time. We can easily forget about order, structure, and routine. Anytime we know what to expect, we can find it easier to live in peace. A child who has suffered the chaos of past trauma thrives in a structured environment, and you set the tone for that structure. Bottom line, if you have a plan, you will experience much more peace than if you didn't. This begins by establishing a routine for your mornings, daytime, nighttime, and bedtime.

Do something that brings you joy. A few years ago, Jayne Schooler from Back2Back Ministries in Ohio and I (Mike) were talking about self-care for us as parents. She said, "I believe doing something that brings us joy is a vital part of self-care." She went on to tell me that it had been years since she played tennis because of having to be so hands-on with her children. But finally she decided to pick up her racket again. It had been years since she stepped onto a court, but the first time she did, the joy of it immediately filled her.

Friend, you need this. Remember that old hobby you used to love? Remember the days of participating in that club or group that filled you? Find something you love to do. It may not be a painting class in Italy, but it might be an online art class that meets after the kids are in bed. Whatever it is, make the effort to do it. You'll be glad you did when you find yourself refreshed and better able to self-regulate on the difficult days.

Be grateful. We can get so hyper-focused on the hard things that we forget to celebrate and give thanks for what we do have. A few years ago, I (Kristin) was in a dark place. I was dealing with depression and anxiety and could not see past the struggle we were having with one of our children. Then my mom told me, "Say thank you for everything, even the little things, even the breath in your lungs." Each word of gratitude releases some of the burden we are carrying. Gratitude is a choice we can make that makes all the difference in our perspectives. On this journey, on our children, and on our lives. When we focus on the things we can be grateful for, we can more easily self-regulate and model that for our children.

Self-Care Isn't Being Selfish

You may want this but are still wrestling with this feeling of selfishness by even thinking about taking better care of you. You may pull out all the excuses for why you can't practice better self-care, but let us give you this insight. Self-care is one of the most giving, selfless things you can do for your family. When you take better care of yourself, you allow yourself the ability to stay regulated and to re-regulate in a healthy way. We know. We've been there. We fought against the thoughts that guilted us into believing we didn't have the time or the right to practice self-care. But when we started putting these practices in place, we discovered it did make our entire family healthier. We're sure that when you put them into practice for yourself, you'll discover the same.

What Now?

- Journal or discuss with a friend:
  - Which three people do you trust, who won't judge you? Keep those names handy for the times you need help.
  - What brings you joy? What is keeping you from pursuing it?
  - What are some ways you can get a few minutes for yourself each day?

Remember . . .

- *Your emotional regulation sets the tone for the rest of your home.*
- *You model how to handle stress and how to re-regulate your own body.*
- *Self-care isn't selfish.*

CHAPTER 13

CO-REGULATION
AND
SELF-REGULATION
STRATEGIES

We know that when a child is in a regulated state, they are at their baseline of emotional well-being. But when they become dysregulated, they often struggle with re-regulating or self-regulating, which means they need help to get back to that baseline of emotional well-being.

Teaching regulation to children who have experienced trauma is not only necessary, it is often complicated. Any time a child experiences trauma, it disrupts the natural pattern of regulation. The natural pattern to self-regulation is learned from before birth when a mother meets the child's needs. They are warm, fed, and safe. Once they are born, their circle of care grows. If a child has a need, they show signs of dysregulation, a caregiver notices these signs and meets the need. When a child experiences trauma, this pattern of need-dysregulation-met need-regulation is disrupted. How can we lead our children to a place of regulation if they have experienced trauma? That's where we step alongside them and help them through co-regulation.

Co-regulation is taking the lead in meeting your child's needs. Co-regulation, at a glance, is helping your child meet a need even if they cannot express it—and it is vitally important to a healthy relationship between children and caregivers. We co-regulate even when our child can't express their own needs. Co-regulation helps build trust and form secure attachments. It also teaches the skills children will need to regulate themselves, or self-regulate, as they mature.

Oftentimes our children's behaviors can escalate quickly. Our children's trauma histories can cause them to revert to their survival brain in times of stress, so our job is to help them return to their logical brain.

Co-regulation always requires a connection. When a child is feeling dysregulated, we need to set the tone for regulation by communicating that we will stay right beside them. The results are not guaranteed, but when we work to connect, we can often bring those quickly escalated behaviors back down. We can do this verbally or with our presence. If we notice our child is feeling anxious, we have the opportunity to say, "It looks like you're feeling anxious. What can I do to help you calm down?" Perhaps our child is struggling to keep their body under control. So they may need to sit on our lap, snuggle close, or receive a hug in order to feel secure.

You may be thinking, *Yeah, but my child pushes me away when I try to connect with him.* When a child is dysregulated, they may not be able to connect with the caregiver. Stay close anyway. Connection must be a part of co-regulation. Connection leads to attachment, and attachment aids in healing and builds the foundation for all relationships and interactions.

Recently, I (Mike) was talking with a friend who felt hopeless about connecting to his child during a meltdown. "She doesn't want me around when she's upset," he said. "I try to ask her what I can do for her, or how I can help her, and she screams, 'I don't want your help!' Do I still try to connect with her?"

"Yes, absolutely," I told him. "But it looks a little different."

Just because the child pushes you away and verbalizes that they don't need or want you doesn't mean this is true. They need you more than ever. While his daughter pushes him away, it's crucial to stay close. He can respond with, "That's okay. I want you to know that if you change your mind, or want to talk to me, I'm right here when you're ready." I reminded him to speak these words in a calm and patient tone.

The following diagram illustrates the escalation and de-escalation of emotional regulation in children and the importance of caregiver regulation as a steady foundation for the child.

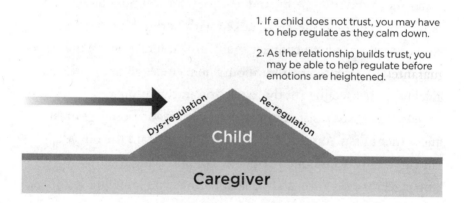

1. If a child does not trust, you may have to help regulate as they calm down.

2. As the relationship builds trust, you may be able to help regulate before emotions are heightened.

Dys-regulation

Re-regulation

Child

Caregiver

Here's an example of dysregulation and the necessary response as it relates to this diagram: Casey becomes anxious every day around lunchtime. A lot of children are in her home, and lunchtime tends to bring chaos. When Casey was very young, she did not have enough food. She often feels the urge to fight with her siblings and take things off their plates. Her foster mother recognizes Casey's past history and the feeling of dysregulation that seems to be triggered by lunchtime. She invites Casey to help her make lunch and gives her a small snack before the other children come into the kitchen. Casey's foster mom is co-regulating with her by staying close, meeting her physical needs, and connecting to her in a fun way.

Sometimes a caregiver does not know the child as well as Casey's foster mom knows her. This caregiver may need to wait until the child begins the process of regulation on her own and then meet her as she is calming down. Co-regulation can also take place in the cool-off period. Casey's foster mom didn't know what was causing Casey's behavior when she first entered the home. Casey would whine and become angry and agitated every day around lunchtime. Whenever she sat at the table with the other children, she would take things off their plates and start fights. These interactions almost always ended with Casey throwing her plate and kicking a chair over, while her foster siblings left the room upset. Casey's foster mom stayed close by, and as Casey was calming down, she helped her clean up the mess, talked with her, and hugged her when she was ready to connect again. This interaction set the stage for Casey to accept her foster mom's help co-regulating at the beginning of her feelings of dysregulation in the future.

Before you can assist your children with regulation, you must know them first. You get to see your children from the outside, which gives you a unique perspective of observing their body language, tone of voice, and behavior. Once you know these things, you can help them regulate and help them to identify their body's warning signs as well. Ask yourself,

What does my child look like when she is dysregulated?

What facial expression is she making?

Do her cheeks get red?

Does she roll her eyes or look away?

What does my child sound like when he's dysregulated?

What is his tone of voice?

Are there any telltale words or phrases he uses?

How does my child feel when she is dysregulated?

Has she complained of a tummy ache?

Does she seem sleepy or agitated?

Is she hungrier or does she lose her appetite?

Observe the situations that cause dysregulation in your children. Then focus on building trust. If you have not built a trusting relationship with the child, you may not be able to co-regulate right away. You may need to allow the behavior to ramp up to its peak and then begin to de-escalate on its own. At that point, you can co-regulate with the child. They still need you to be present. This is a time you can begin to earn their trust.

1. If a child does not trust, you may have to help regulate as they calm down.

2. As the relationship builds trust, you may be able to help regulate before emotions are heightened.

Dys-regulation → Child ← Re-regulation

Caregiver

As the child has reached the peak of dysregulation, you will notice signs that they are calming down. For instance, their tone of voice may go from high-pitched to hushed. Their shoulders drop from a heightened state. They may stop moving uncontrollably and relax their body. A few years ago, we were on a family trip to North Dakota when one of our children became dysregulated from the long car ride. While we needed to stop for a break, we were in the middle of nowhere with no facilities to use. Kristin was driving, and I was riding in the passenger seat. I recognized our child had become dysregulated (which was easy—the loud swearing gave him away!) and I asked how I could help him. He wouldn't answer me for some time, but finally he asked for his weighted blanket. As I placed the weighted blanket over him, I could see his body relax. After a half hour or so, he was completely re-regulated.

Use an assuring, gentle tone of voice to let the child know you are there. We may say something like, "Hey, sweet girl, I can see you are becoming a little anxious. That's okay. But here's what I want you to know. There's plenty of food here, and I will make sure you get enough." This reinforces re-regulation and establishes language to use with the feelings of dysregulation. As we begin to build trust, we may be able to move our level of assistance back toward the beginning of the dysregulation in the future.

Here's the most important piece of this diagram as it relates to us: *the caregiver must remain regulated throughout the process of co-regulation.* Remember, we provide the baseline for the child to regulate. You and I set the tone through our own voice, body language, and actions. We'll talk more about this in the next chapter.

Co-regulation Strategies Based on Ages

Let's consider some specific examples of co-regulation, based on a child's age.

Infants through Toddlers

It is important to begin with co-regulation strategies for infants first. If we can filter our understanding of co-regulation through the lens of raising an infant, we can more readily adapt these strategies to older children. When an infant is showing signs of distress, we have some natural responses as caregivers, which ensure the child's needs are met. We don't often stop to ponder the behavior; instead, we jump to action. We pick up the baby, hold them, use a soft tone, make eye contact, rock them gently. Then we ask ourselves questions in an attempt to identify the cause of the discomfort. "When did the child eat last? Is the child too warm or too cold? Does the child have a dirty diaper?" When we are caring for an infant, it is unnatural to assume the child is misbehaving. We also don't ask the infant what is wrong, or assume that the infant should be trying harder to stop fussing. We simply know it is our responsibility to meet the child's needs. We meet those needs without resentment. We also attend to an infant's needs with an inherent understanding that our posture, facial expressions, and tone of voice are important. We know without much thought that this caregiving is building trust with the infant.

If we are co-regulating with an infant, we do this by meeting needs first. We make sure the infant has food, sleep, a clean diaper, and appropriate clothing for the temperature. Once we are sure we have met the child's needs, we begin to attend to their emotional needs. We make our presence known by staying close, talking to the baby, and making eye contact. We let very little, if any, time pass while the child is distraught. We will swaddle the baby, wrapping them in a physical feeling of safety. We may also swing the baby or rock in a straight line. It is natural for us to use our voice in a hushed high tone. Even if the newborn is taking a long time to calm down, we will walk with them, sing to them, give them a warm bath, and continue attending to their needs even when we have become frustrated. We don't quit because of that frustration.

Preschool through Elementary Age

Co-regulation becomes more intentional with older children. A preschooler still needs us to tie his shoes or fix him a snack, but he does not need our help in the bathroom. An older-elementary-aged child will not need us to do any of those things, but they still need us to drive them to school, cook their meals, and tuck them into bed at night. Co-regulation with an older child will take a little more creativity than with a newborn. When we notice dysregulation, we must first strive to meet our child's physical needs.

Ask yourself if the child is hungry, tired, or uncomfortable, then assist them in meeting this need. Then ask yourself how you can meet their emotional needs. For instance, you may notice your child is feeling overly excited and short-tempered. They may be crying at a moment's notice or laughing uncontrollably, or both. You realize they didn't have a good night's sleep the night before. So you can run a warm bath, find their favorite pajamas, and offer to read a story. You are co-regulating by helping the child get ready to go to sleep.

While you are helping them get ready, you open the conversation to talk about how they are feeling. You might fill the bath with bubbles and sit on the side of the tub while they bathe. Though they might not need much help, you are staying close by and connected. As you are talking, you say something like, "I noticed you were crying and laughing a lot a little bit ago. How are you feeling now?"

You might find out that your child's friend wasn't nice to them at school earlier. Use this time to listen. You may offer ideas while you talk, like "Did you sleep well last night?" The child may say, "Yes, I'm not tired, that's not what's going on. I'm just mad at my friend." That's okay. This isn't the time to be right; this is the time to get connected. Remember that everything you are doing in this scenario is to help them get ready for bed so they will feel better the next day. Co-regulating with a young child is all about staying connected, providing comfort, and allowing the child to participate in bringing regulation.

Preteen through Teenagers

We often like to joke with our own teens that we're going to help them regulate by swaddling them, feeding them a bottle, or rocking with them in our arms. This usually makes them laugh, but there is actually some truth to the need to co-regulate with older children in the same way we regulate with infants, preschool, and elementary-age children. We aren't really going to swaddle our teenagers, and we aren't going to kneel down on their level (mostly because we can usually look them directly in the eye), but we can take some of the same steps. When we see an older child dysregulated, we need to remind ourselves to respond to the behavior in the same way we would with an infant or young child. We are going to ask ourselves, what is causing this child to feel discomfort? What can I do to meet their physical and emotional needs?

Speaking in a calm and gentle tone is also important. Much like with a child who is in preschool, asking questions like, "What can I do for you?" or "Looks like you're upset about something. What can I do to help you?" helps the teenager know you are there for them.

It's important to note that there are times when you must help your preteen or teenager form words that they are not able to communicate on their own. The reason this is important is that, oftentimes, teenagers who have experienced disrupted or broken attachment in their development turn inward with thoughts and feelings. Then those feelings fester. They become overwhelmed. Their emotions, feelings, and deep needs are like a soda bottle shaken up and ready to explode at the slightest turn of the bottle cap. Then they begin to spill out in ways that become harmful to others, or even themselves.

Casey is a smart, talented, and ultra-creative nineteen-year-old who is working to finish her senior year of high school and move to college. She has been in her parents' care for nearly two decades. They fostered her when she was an infant, and that quickly led to a finalized adoption after parental rights were terminated. As Casey grew into a teenager, one thing became glaringly clear. In many situations where Casey had a need, she would reject her parents' help, and anyone else she was close to. She always attempted to do things on her own. Casey's rejection of help became so severe that she often found herself overwhelmed by everyday tasks, like getting ready for school on time, remembering to check the oil level in her car, or remembering to put her homework in her backpack and not leaving it strewn across the dining-room table. This came across to her family and friends as anger and frustration toward them. Most of the time, no one even knew that Casey needed help. She had convinced herself that she needed to "go at it on her own," because she felt she couldn't count on anyone!

Her words said she didn't need anyone, but her body language and facial expressions told a different story. Her parents inquired about this behavior with a therapist, since they were tired of her rejecting them. The therapist gave them this advice: "You need to help her verbalize her thoughts and feelings when you can tell something's wrong or she has a need. She bottles things up and then they come out as attacks or angst against you and your other kids, which isn't healthy for anyone, including her." The therapist explained that, in normal situations with teenagers who were so close to adulthood, the caregiver may need to step back and give space. Casey needed space too, but she wasn't sure how to navigate it. Casey's parents needed to help her talk through her emotions about growing up. They needed to be intentional about connecting with her even as she did things for herself. They could do this by visiting her at work, praising her hard work in school, and inviting her to do grown-up things like meet for coffee.

Moving Forward with Co-regulation

Meeting an infant's needs is natural but should we really do this for older children too? If a baby is screaming, we don't think twice about feeding them. If an older child is melting down, it often feels like spoiling if we offer them a snack. What if the behavior is a voice that hasn't quite learned to speak the language of emotion? What if the child's behavior is simply telling you that they have an unmet need that they don't know how to express or meet themselves?

For me (Kristin) this was one of the hardest things to learn. If I was screaming at the age of eight, my parents told me to stop screaming or I would suffer a consequence. This was fair, especially since I had experienced co-regulation from the time I was born. I knew my needs would be met and I knew the language needed to express my needs. If I was screaming at the age of eight, there might have been something really wrong or I might have just been mad at my sister. If the latter, my parents were right to demand I stop screaming. I knew better and I had better skills. Children who have not consistently had their needs met and who don't know the language needed to express those needs may revert to survival behaviors. As caregivers, we must return ourselves to the perspective we would have with an infant.

We must go back to the way trust and attachment happens naturally in infancy, first by meeting physical needs and then by meeting emotional needs. An older child can learn to co-regulate and eventually self-regulate when a consistent, trustworthy caregiver gives the time and patience to teach the child to build up their feelings of safety.

Below, consider these common scenarios in which the ability and willingness to help a child emotionally regulate could drastically change the outcome.

Meet Your Child at Their Level

We need to get on the child's level. For a younger child, we may crouch down next to them so we are on the same level as them. With an older child, we may pull up a chair and sit near them or stand at a safe distance while our bodies are turned toward them in an open pose (arms unfolded, legs uncrossed or crossed toward the child). Recently, one of our teenagers was lying on the sofa at the end of a difficult day and lots of dysregulation. I (Mike) sat next to her on the sofa and talked with her in a soft tone. You could see her body relax as we spoke.

Make Eye Contact

Helping our children look at us in the eye strengthens their ability to trust. This does not have to be prolonged eye contact. Just a quick glance, eye to eye, will help you and them feel connected. You may say, "May I see your eyes please?" Then wait. As soon as the child glances at you, say, "Thank you." Or you might say, "Hey, do you know what color my eyes are?" As soon as they look, smile. With a younger child, you may feel it is appropriate to say something silly like, "Hey, is there a purple dot on my face?" A glance is all you need.

Use Humor

Humor goes a long way toward co-regulation with a child. You know the child you are working with the best. If you know they will find something funny, share it with them. Let's imagine you are already on the level of the child, you have made eye contact, and then you say, "Did I ever tell you about the time I tripped over my own feet in front of the entire middle school?" or "Oh my goodness, did you hear what my new puppy did the other day?"

Humor has a way of transforming our emotions. We can feel closer to regulation just by having a good laugh. This may not always work. One of our children absolutely cannot laugh when they are feeling dysregulated. Sometimes we make the mistake of trying to tell a joke or be silly when this child isn't feeling great. When we make that mistake, we apologize right away and save the silliness for later.

Try Distraction and Transitional Objects

Though distraction won't make the root of the issue go away, it can be just the thing to reset a child's brain so it can more quickly return to logical thinking and reasoning. Distraction can be just about anything. We may offer the child a snack or drink. We may ask the child a question unrelated to the situation at hand, such as, "Have you seen the new Avengers movie?" or "I'm about to get a soda—do you want one too?" or "I think I'm going to take the dog for a walk. Want to grab her treats and come along?"

Fidgets are a great way to access a part of the brain that isn't able to be accessed during time of distress. Handing them an object they may be interested in can help them move from the survival brain into another part of the brain without even knowing it. This could be something like a piece of Play-Doh or modeling clay. It could be a twist tie, a smelly marker, a soft toy, or a bouncy ball. This may feel like bribing or spoiling. But fidgets shouldn't be used as a bribe; they should be used and viewed as a tool. You wouldn't hesitate to give your child a spoon to eat a jar of applesauce or a jacket to get warm. Don't hesitate to hand them something to fidget with while their brains are trying to return to their baseline.

You can use transitional objects when a child is doing something or entering a situation that is making them feel uncomfortable. A transitional object can be anything—a special blanket or their caregiver's sweatshirt or pillow that a child takes to bed with them, or a coin to keep in their pocket that they can touch if they're feeling anxious. A transitional object can be a heart drawn on the palm of a child's hand that they can squeeze if they feel nervous. It can also be a favorite pair of socks, the hoodie pulled up on a sweatshirt, or an undershirt that makes the child feel secure. The object needs to be attached to a positive emotion, memory, or guarantee. For instance, "I was thinking you might like to sleep with Mommy's sweatshirt while I'm out of town so you remember that Mommy will be back before you know it." A transitional object can be used as a way to co-regulate with your child when you can't be physically present. It requires thinking ahead and being creative. Mommy can't sleep with the child or stay with the child at school but she can remind the child of her presence with an object.

Provide Weighted Objects

The weight of a blanket, lap pad, or wrap gives proprioceptive input to the child's body. In simple terms, it feels like a hug. A child may be able to accept this type of security before he can receive it from a caregiver. Weighted products are not to be used all the time; rather, they should be used as a tool to help the body regulate. But as they use it, you co-regulate with them by remaining near them. Note that not all weighted products are created equally. Do some research before you purchase one for your child.

Offer Food or Water

Recently, one of our children became dysregulated not long before bedtime. As we were conversing with him, (I) Kristin asked if he'd like a snack. The snack met his underlying need of hunger, helped him turn his mind from the dysregulation, and gave an opportunity for him to feel secure and willing to get his mind and body re-regulated.

Food and water are foundations for our physical health and well-being. A child who has experienced food insecurity may always need a reminder that plenty of food is available. Even a child who has a healthy relationship with food can be comforted and connected within the presence of food. Remember that much of the bonding we do with infants happens around feeding. From that time on, food is an important part of our physical well-being as well as our emotional connectedness. When you are co-regulating with a child, connecting over a cup of hot chocolate or a plate of fries will be an enjoyable experience for you both.

Stay with Them

Several years ago, our child needed a cool-down (which is an alternative to a time-out), and I (Mike) offered to sit next to him. Sit beside a child who has trouble regulating. You may not always be able to assist but you can sit close by. Have a child join you in the kitchen while making dinner or walk with you to the mailbox to get the mail. If you cannot get the child to come with you somewhere, go to them. You may need to pause what you're doing and read a book in the corner of their room while they fall asleep or bring your own work to the dining-room table, joining them while they work on a difficult homework assignment.

Provide Physical Contact

Hug, hold, or squeeze a child who enjoys physical contact. We have a child who loves to receive or give "powerful" hugs. As this child is getting older, we have to remind him not to squeeze too hard! He loves the feeling of deep pressure. Another of our children asks us just about every evening if we will rub his back. As we do, he always asks if we will, in his words, "push harder" on his back. He loves the deep pressure feeling of our hands on his back. You may press on the child's shoulders, rub their back, sit close on the couch, or hold their hand.

Offer Comforting Tactile Objects

Is the child sensitive to certain textures? Help the child choose clothing, blankets, outerwear, headphones, and even utensils that feel good to them. If your child is a sensory seeker or someone who likes a variety of textures, help them choose something that makes them feel good when they feel dysregulated. This can be offering them their favorite sweatshirt to cuddle up in, or putting a blanket in the dryer for a few minutes and wrapping it around their shoulders. Then when they are trying to re-regulate, you can offer them that object to help them in the process.

Give Them Space

Giving space doesn't really seem like a co-regulation strategy, but it is also an important part of letting your child know you are secure in yourself and able to be patient enough to allow them to work through their emotions. You may give your child space while they are re-regulating with the understanding that you will be close by. You may say, "I see you need a little space. It's okay with me for you to choose to ride your bike for a bit. I'm going to check on you in five minutes and see how you are doing." For a teen, you may say, "I know you need your space and I respect that. I'm cool with you staying in your room for a bit. Because I love you, I'll check on you in thirty minutes and see how you're doing."

Moving toward Self-Regulation

Coming full circle with the child is important. We need to allow the child to begin to take ownership over their own body and mind. When they see they can regulate their emotions, they become more willing to handle undesirable situations and emotions in the future. How do we move them toward self-regulation? Here are some ways to start:

Teach Emotional Language

Our children learn a lot by what they see modeled. So if we want them to learn to self-regulate, we must model appropriate re-regulation skills for them. When our children hear us using our words to describe our feelings and emotions, they become comfortable using their words as well.

Talking through meeting our physical needs can lead to verbalizing our emotional needs. I might say something like, "I have a presentation at work today. I'm feeling nervous about it. I had a hard time sleeping last night, and my stomach feels upset. I think I'm going to do something to help myself feel regulated. I'm going to try to eat a healthy breakfast and then I'm going to try to refocus on my notes again." Or I might say, "I had a hard time sleeping. I was tossing and turning all night. I think I'm worried about my presentation at work today. I think I'm going to take a warm shower, get my best work clothes on, and give myself a reset."

As caregivers we can use words that describe feelings of emotional regulation and familiarize our children with them. Once those conversations become part of our everyday language, we can refer back to those dialogues. We may say, "Remember that time I was so nervous about my presentation at work? It made my tummy feel upset and I had trouble sleeping. I think you may be feeling that way too. Are you worried about the field trip at school today? When I was feeling nervous, a shower helped me feel better. What things might make you feel better?"

We have a child who rubs his eye when he's anxious, angry, nervous, or excited. He rubs his eyes so hard that we worry he's going to cause damage. We now know, though, that eye rubbing is a warning sign that our child is above or below the baseline of regulation.

I (Kristin) observed him rubbing his eye, so I began the conversation. "I noticed you were feeling really anxious about starting school today and you rubbed at your eye really hard. Did you notice that?" Then I dug deeper. "What are some things you noticed about yourself today?"

"I felt sick to my stomach. My arms felt shaky and I wasn't sure I wanted to eat lunch," he admitted.

I nodded and listened.

He said, "I felt sleepy and all I could think about was getting home and watching television. I started rubbing my eyes a lot, and my new teacher asked if there was something in my eye. You know what? I do that a lot when I feel nervous."

I continued to nod. "I've noticed that too," I said. "How interesting." My job here was not to be the expert on my child. It was to teach him to be an expert about himself.

Help your child know emotion words. Remember that any emotion above or below the baseline is dysregulation. This may mean that a child who is really excited to go to a birthday party may feel dysregulated. A child who is anxious about spending the night at a friend's house may feel dysregulated. A child who is giddy on Christmas morning or sleepless the night before a big test is feeling dysregulated.

We tend to be lazy with words in the English language. We "love" pizza and we "love our spouse." These are two very different types of love, but we use the same word. Emotions can be the same way. Learning many different ways to describe our emotions can help us and our children to zero in on a better understanding.

Angry can also be annoyed, bitter, enraged, exasperated, furious, heated, impassioned, indignant, irate, irritable, irritated, offended, outraged, resentful, sullen, uptight, antagonized, displeased, affronted, cross, turbulent, maddened.

Sad can also be bitter, dismal, heartbroken, melancholy, mournful, pessimistic, somber, sorrowful, sorry, wistful, bereaved, blue, cheerless, dejected, despairing, despondent, disconsolate, distressed, down, downcast, forlorn, gloomy, glum, grief-stricken, grieved, heartsick, heavyhearted, hurting, troubled, morose, low.

Anxious can also be afraid, apprehensive, careful, concerned, distressed, fearful, fidgety, jittery, envious, restless, scared, uneasy, uptight, antsy, disquieted, disturbed, fretful, hyper, jumpy, overwrought, shaky, troubled, wired.

Frustrated can also be cramped, defeated, discontented, discouraged, disheartened, embittered, irked, resentful, ungratified.

Happy can also be cheerful, contented, delighted, ecstatic, elated, glad, joyful, joyous, jubilant, lively, merry, overjoyed, peaceful, pleased, thrilled, upbeat, blissful, blithe, chipper, content, gleeful, jolly, light, mirthful, playful, peppy.

Excited can also be agitated, annoyed, delighted, eager, enthusiastic, hysterical, nervous, passionate, thrilled, animated, aroused, awakened, charged, inflamed, provoked, roused, ruffled, stimulated, wired, fired up, frantic, hyperactive.

Each of these words are synonyms, but they each carry a different meaning, reaction, and understanding. Words are important. Teaching ourselves and our children to use a variety of words will bring power over handling emotions.

We need to encourage our children to use feeling words. Sometimes this will be uncomfortable for all of us but the more we practice, the more we will become comfortable with feeling a variety of emotions and sitting with each other through them.

As you practice emotion words, also identify where you are feeling those emotions. Ask your child, "Where are you feeling that in your body?" A child who is anxious or scared may feel a tingling in the legs or back. They may feel an upset stomach or a pain in their eye. Our body is connected to our emotions in every way. When we can identify that something feels different in our body, we can follow the clues to get to the root of the change. Using these clues can help us take power over our body's reaction.

Ask your child, "How does your heart or soul feel?" This is different from but still connected to the body. This feeling is our sense of self, our place in this world. A child may respond with feeling words like *sad*, *excited*, or *peaceful* to describe their state of being.

Finally, encourage your child to describe what they are feeling in their mind. I (Kristin) sometimes say, "What is your brain telling you right now?" My child may respond, "My brain is telling me that I'm stupid and I'm never going to understand math." Or he might say, "My brain says I'm a good kid and I work hard even when math is difficult." The child is still dealing with the same difficulty but his brain is reacting in two different ways.

Help Them Communicate Needs

Remember that communicating needs begins in early childhood. A caregiver may notice a newborn crying, so the caregiver picks up the baby and says, "Shh, it's okay. I think you may be hungry. I'm going to fix you a bottle," all the while rocking and comforting that baby. "Here is your bottle," the caregiver says and gives the baby the bottle. "Yum, that's good, isn't it? You are feeling a lot better now, I can tell." Does the caregiver engage in this dialogue because they believe the baby will respond or that the baby will take a hint and fix themselves a bottle? Of course not. A caregiver naturally engages in this conversation, which will one day lead to the child taking ownership of their own self-care and self-regulation.

When our children start to create this dialogue for themselves, it's time for us to listen and encourage. Our child may say something like "I'm so angry, you always make me go to bed early. It's not fair, I hate you. You aren't my real mom anyway." If we respond with, "Wow, you seem really angry and frustrated. What is going on?" we have just opened the door for the child to dig deeper. He may respond, "I'm mad that I have to go to bed—bed is stupid . . . and scary."

He has just given us a clue, and we can dig even deeper. "What seems scary about bed?" The child may respond, "The monster is going to get me when you turn out the light."

We didn't know anything about the "monster" until now so we can ask more questions. "What monster?"

The child feels heard, validated, and curious about himself. "I think there might be a monster. I read a scary book at the library today and I've been worried all day about it."

We didn't know any of that until we asked the questions, but now that we do, we can further encourage the child to think through his emotions. "I didn't know anything about that book or the monster. I think you must be feeling afraid. Books can do that to us sometimes, even to me. Let's have a look under your bed. I am 100 percent sure there is nothing there, but I think it might make you feel better if we take a look together."

As the child's fears settle, we can bring the conversation full circle. "I don't think you were really mad at me tonight, but your words came out that way. What can you do next time you're feeling that way?"

As our children practice this skill with us, they will become competent at meeting their needs for themselves, therefore self-regulating. Eventually, our children will say things like, "I'm feeling nervous about applying to college. I think I'd like to become a teacher, but I don't know that I have what it takes. I'm really doubting myself. I think I am going to shadow a couple of local teachers and get a better feel for what their job is like. I also think I'm going to visit a couple of college campuses and see if I can picture myself living there." A child can now carry this skill into adulthood. This adult will now be able to walk into difficult situations while keeping their body and mind regulated.

———————————— **What Now?** ————————————

- Journal or discuss with a friend:
  - What behaviors have you witnessed with your children that point toward the need for co-regulation?
  - What needs can you better help to meet with your child through co-regulation strategies?
  - How can you begin to make co-regulation a regular practice when your child is dysregulated?
  - What are some ways you can encourage your child to self-regulate?

Remember . . .

- *Co-regulation requires connection and is the foundation for self-regulation later.*
- *When trust has been damaged by trauma, co-regulation will become even more necessary, especially when it's difficult.*
- *The goal is for children to take ownership of their re-regulation.*

WHAT TO DO WHEN . . . ?

By now you're probably thinking, *This is too much to take in! What do I do when my child is flipping out in the back seat of the van, and I'm only making it worse?* Or, *How do I know if my son's behavior is insecurity speaking and not him wanting to ruin every good thing I try to give him?* We understand. We can't even begin to count how many times we've discovered a new concept or idea and immediately wondered, *How do I actually do that?*

We recognize that although throughout the book we offer insight and practical help, you may still have a question about dysregulation. We've included below a few more challenges that we often hear about from parents and help for you to navigate these tricky situations.

My Child Feels Insecure

One of our deepest needs as humans is to feel secure. One of our greatest struggles as foster and adoptive families is the feeling of insecurity. Insecurity is what led to the situation that required the foster or adoptive placement. A child who has lost his first mother and father is going to feel insecure. This insecurity will lead to dys-regulation. In order to move our child back into a state of regula-tion, we must first address the insecurity and meet the needs to the best of our ability. Here are a few concerns our child may have.

Worry about a Caregiver

We live in an amazingly connected world. If your child is strug-gling while at school, talk to the school about creating a plan to call home during the day. Help the school understand how this simple connection can ease your child's mind and help them refocus for the rest of the day. Send your child to school or childcare with a transitional object, such as your sweater or a family picture. You can use anything as a transitional object—the importance comes when you assign meaning to the object. For instance, you can get a penny, kiss the penny, and put it in your child's pocket, and then tell them to reach in their pocket and rub the penny if they get worried.

Your child may feel this type of dysregulation at bedtime. Allow your child to take your pillow to bed or start out in your bed. Your child may be worried about a biological family member. Do your best to ease these fears by staying connected to the family member in any way you can. Phone calls and letters are great. Visits can be wonderful. If you can't have that kind of contact, use the transi-tional object as a way to stay connected. Tuck a picture under your child's pillow or give them a bracelet with their family member's birthstone.

Housing

Housing is another of our most basic needs as humans. For many of our children, housing has been unstable, unpredictable, or unsafe. Your child may feel insecure about the home you live in, especially during times of political unrest, war, or seasons of natu-ral disaster. Every year during tornado season, one of our children becomes obsessed with tornado safety. He runs through scenarios with me (Kristin) about what we will do if we lose our house. Where we will live. How much we might lose in terms of money and belongings. This child is fascinated by weather, but it is also important to remember that this child spent a significant amount of time during his first years of life in a homeless shelter. He has stored the memory of housing insecurity in his mind and body. Tornado season is a trigger of a past memory.

We can begin when children are very young teaching them about home ownership, rent, banks, jobs, and bills. Oftentimes we believe that we should keep these things from our children because they are grown-up concepts. Our children have already experienced many things that are too "grown up" for you and me even to comprehend. They are smart and intuitive. Invite your child to help you pay the bills. Show them how the meter reader measures the amount of electricity you use. Help them open a bank account and practice depositing money and checking the balance; use that money to give, save, and spend. Allow them to help create the family values and expectations. Write these out and sign them. Hang them on your wall for everyone to see. There is power in knowledge and there is security in participating in the ownership of the home.

Food Insecurity

Food insecurity is an issue a child who has experienced it will not soon forget. His or her body will remember the feeling of hunger, and the survival brain will often take over without warning. Waiting for lunchtime at school or a change in schedule that makes a mealtime late can be especially difficult. Do your best to set meals at regular times and allow for frequent snacks. Pack your child a backpack filled with snacks that they can carry with them at all times. Talk with your child's school about their food insecurity and see if the teacher or school nurse can keep some special snacks for the child to have if they are feeling hungry or worried about food. Keep a bowl of snacks that are okay to have anytime. Use language around food that promotes security, such as, "I know you feel hungry. Dinner is in fifteen minutes. Will you help me stir the veggies?" or "Remember, we have plenty of food. Let's look in the refrigerator together and see what we would like to make for your after-school snack today."

I'm the Cause of Dysregulation

We're exhausted, so it makes perfect sense that our emotions can often get the best of us. Sometimes we aren't emotionally regulated. Sometimes we are the cause of our child's dysregulation. When this is the case, we need to do a few things.

Apologize

The first and best place to start is to apologize. Own what you need to own, get down on your child's level, look them in the eyes, and apologize for what happened. Even if it's excruciating, even if you don't feel apologetic. Remember, this is about building and repairing broken trust and disrupted attachment. Children with a trauma history often have an inability to understand actions and consequences.

Reconnect

Since our children often function out of survival, they can be quick to disconnect from us when we have wronged them. It's our child's way of saying, *I'll reject you before you can reject me further. I'll disconnect from you before I face being wounded any deeper.* To the best of our ability as caregivers, we need to take intentional steps to reconnect with our children after we've wronged them. This needs to be immediate. Last year, I (Mike) reacted harshly to one of my son's behaviors. I raised my voice, my tone was sharp, and I said things I regretted instantly. He was sad and angry and stormed off to his room. After a minute or two and some deep breaths, I followed him, and we spent the next thirty minutes talking, hugging, and reconnecting.

Reconcile

Several years ago, I (Mike) lost my temper and said some mean things to one of my children. She burst into tears and ran to her bedroom where she stayed the rest of the night. Kristin advised that I give her time to cool off, which was wise. The next morning when she came downstairs, I looked her in the eyes and apologized for the words I'd said to her. It would take more than just saying I was sorry to reinforce the apology, but I knew my first and most important step with my daughter was to reconcile and tell her how sorry I was. Reconciliation is about taking the necessary steps to change patterns with your children. Reconciliation is not only about apologizing, but about making things right by changing our behavioral patterns.

Reframe

In order to fix what you and I have broken with our children, we must reframe our words, our actions, and our reactions. Reframing requires us to evaluate how we ask our children questions, how we verbally respond to their behaviors, and how we react to certain situations with them that may be out of our control. We don't have control over the world around us but we do have control over our tone, reaction, body, and words. Reframing requires us to demolish our old way of parenting our children, and rebuild our approach, sometimes entirely.

My Child Is Unsafe in the Car

One of the most common questions we receive from parents is, "How do I keep my child safe in the car?" If your child has difficulty riding safely in the car, here are a few things you can do.

Use a Large Car Seat

If your child is beyond the toddler years, but routinely unbuckles himself in the car, it may be time to purchase a large car seat. When our foster son was nine, we took this measure to help him feel safe and secure in the car. This child sat in the large car seat until he was twelve. It started as a preventative measure to stop him from jumping out of a moving car, but it ended up creating a feeling of safety and security for him, which solved much of the dangerous behavior from the root of the problem—impulsivity and insecurity. These can be purchased at a safety store, your local children's hospital, online, or wherever adaptive equipment is sold. The car seat will provide a physical sense of safety for the child, the straps are a little more difficult to unbuckle, and it may feel more comfortable to travel for the child.

Plan Ahead

If we know that car rides can be triggers for our children, and we cannot avoid trips to the grocery, the pediatrician, or school, it's crucial that we plan ahead. Planning ahead begins with discussions about the upcoming car ride. These may have to be lengthy discussions at first. Our children often need a lot of time and space to re-orient their brains. They can often be triggered simply because they haven't been given adequate mental space to change directions. So it's up to us to enter into conversations about what we have planned.

Start way before you have to leave: "Sweet girl, you can have a snack and watch a show, but I want you to know that in an hour, we have to take a car ride to the grocery." And then remind her every ten minutes of the upcoming change. This will help her make the change mentally.

You may also want to prepare by bringing a snack with you in the car, especially if you have to leave right when she gets home from school or soon after the activity she is engaged in. Have the snack ready to go in a small snack baggy. Along with a planned snack, bring some calming activities for her to do in the car. Bring books, her favorite toys, an iPad (if she's allowed to have screen time), headphones, or fidgets. Bring her into the conversation of what activities she'd like to have in the car. Doing this in advance is a technique that will help her turn the corner mentally and adjust to the change of having to take a car ride.

Finally, as you discuss the change of taking a car ride to the grocery, walk her through your goals for the trip. "We have to get our groceries for the week so we can make yummy meals for everyone! How does that sound?" Or, "We have to make this trip so we can get all of the yummy foods we like. What kind of meals would you like to have this week?" This brings her in on your goal and allows her to have ownership over the process.

Pull Over If You Need To

Your number-one goal is safety. Children are not safe in the car if they are unbuckled. Pull over, if you need to. Plan for extra time to pull over and re-regulate before you resume your drive.

Take Separate Cars

Oftentimes children become dysregulated by other children. This is never more the case than in the confines of a car. We have personally found that taking two cars, with one of us in one car alone with the child who is easily triggered, provides a much safer, and often, efficient ride. Plus, in the event that we do have to pull the car over until the child re-regulates, it will not disrupt the other children's car ride. We have spent years driving to church, the park, friends' houses, and family gatherings in multiple cars. If you're in a co-parenting situation, and have means to take more than one car, you may need to do this for a season or two. Yes, it's a headache, and yes, it costs extra money, but we've found that we simply can't put a price tag on safety or peace.

I Have Trouble Co-regulating My Child

Below we have listed common scenarios in which the ability of and willingness to help a child emotionally regulate could drastically change the outcome.

Dsyregulation in the Classroom

Scenario #1: Mr. Smith teaches sixth-grade math. In his classroom, students are not allowed to wear hoodies or hats. One day while Mr. Smith is teaching a new concept, he notices that David is wearing his hoodie. Mr. Smith calls out from the front of the classroom, "David, you know you aren't allowed to wear a hoodie. Take it off right now and return it to your locker." David shrinks into his seat and pulls the hood tighter around his face. Mr. Smith walks quickly toward David and stands over his desk. "Look at me right now, David." David continues to stare at his desk, refusing to make eye contact. "If you do not look me in the eyes right now and take that hoodie off, I will call the resource officer," Mr. Smith says. David begins to cry, pulling the hoodie over his eyes. Mr. Smith walks to the front of the classroom and picks up the phone to dial the resource officer. The officer arrives in less than a minute, walks to David's desk, and tells him to take off the hoodie. David grips the sides of the desk, and the officer threatens to remove him from the classroom by force. David does not budge, and the officer forcibly removes David while David begins to scream and kick.

In this scenario, the teacher wanted immediate obedience with minimal disruption to his class. What he got was a disruption that cost nearly twenty minutes of teaching time, loss of focus from his other students, and loss of dignity for the child with the hoodie.

What if the teacher had addressed the child's state of emotional regulation first? Would the outcome have been different? Possibly. Here is what this scenario might have looked like.

Scenario #2: The teacher notices David has his hoodie pulled over his ears. He asks himself, *Is David feeling insecure or maybe even cold? Is the noise level in the classroom bothering him?* Once Mr. Smith tries to see David's perspective, he might have also evaluated what he knows about David's auditory processing disorder (noted in his IEP) as well as David's exposure to childhood trauma, and organic brain damage due to a stroke he suffered as an infant. He may remind himself the police forcibly removed David from his first family when he was little. He might even ask himself how he would have reacted when he was twelve to having a teacher call him out in front of the class. These observations might change Mr. Smith's reaction.

In the second scenario, Mr. Smith makes a quick observation first, then makes a plan. He waits until David looks up at him and then he quickly makes a gesture imitating the removal of the hoodie, then smiles and nods in approval when David removes the hood. Or Mr. Smith walks toward David's desk and crouches at eye level, talking in a soft voice: "I'm sorry, David, I can't let you wear that in class—please take the hood off. Thank you." Or Mr. Smith could write a message on a sticky note, "Please take your hoodie off, thanks," and put it on David's desk and walk away. Or Mr. Smith could use a cheerful tone of voice—"David, hoodie, thanks," keeping directions simple, straightforward, and nonthreatening. The outcome in this situation would be very different. David might still refuse, but it is unlikely. David's behavior in scenario #1 was largely a reaction to the feeling of embarrassment, shame, confusion, and fear.

Dysregulation in the Car

Scenario #1: Bella and her family are about to drive home from Grandma's house in Ohio after spending a few days with her over Christmas break. They only visit once in the summer and once during the holidays. Bella loves her grandmother. It's a three-hour trip. After fueling up the car, grabbing a coffee at Starbucks, and throwing away some lingering trash, Bella's parents turn onto the expressway and head for home. For the first thirty minutes, everything is peaceful and calm. Suddenly from the back seat, their oldest child says, "Stop, Bella!" Another twenty seconds goes by and again, "I said *stop!*" Bella snaps back, "I'm not doing anything to you!" But her parents have heard this before. Her parents persist with the drive, but a few miles farther, Bella is throwing things from the back of the car to the front, she is unbuckled from her seat, and screaming, "I hate this family!" at the top of her lungs. Bella's mom is tired. This is an everyday occurrence during car rides and she's over it. She responds to Bella out of exhaustion. "Sit down, buckle your seat belt, or you will watch everyone else eat their McDonald's when we stop and you will have nothing!" Bella continues to escalate. "Shut up!" she yells at her mom. Mom responds, "You will *not* talk to me that way, young lady. One more word like that, and I will take your bag of toys away, and you'll have nothing to do for the next three hours." Bella holds her ground, and so does her mother. The dysregulation continues for the rest of the drive.

Or let's consider *scenario #2:* Bella begins to melt down on the car ride home from her grandma's house. Her mother asks herself a crucial question: *What's really going on with Bella?* If we trace it back to the surrounding circumstances, a lot is going on and has been going on with Bella's family. First of all, it's Christmas. The season between October 31 and January 1 tends to be massively overstimulating with trick-or-treating, family gatherings, twinkling lights, Santa Claus, presents, lots of food dye and sugar. Bella's mother realizes Bella is overstimulated by the holidays and simply doesn't know what to do with her feelings of excitement and her disappointment over having to leave Grandma's. Her mother also knows that car rides are difficult and this one will be tough because it's long. She asks, "Bella, what's happening? You seem like something's bothering you. Is there something I can do to help?" She realizes how Bella is feeling and offers to stop early for dinner at McDonald's, then invites Bella to watch for the correct exit. Once Bella is feeling better, her mother reminds her of appropriate behavior: "I'm glad you're feeling better. Now, I want you to know that it's not okay to touch people or to make people upset with our words. You need to make things right with your siblings. One thing you can do is help them by cleaning up all of their trash from dinner."

Dysregulation at Bedtime

Scenario #1: Jenifer has taken a bath, read a story with her mother, and brushed her teeth. As she is about to get into bed, she suddenly tells her mother she needs to go to the bathroom one more time. Jenifer's mother sighs and says okay. After the bathroom, Jenifer climbs into bed but then asks for a drink of water. Her mother obliges but she's getting frustrated. Jenifer's voice takes on a whining tone. She begins to baby talk. Her mother says, "That is enough, Jenifer. Go to bed." Jenifer whimpers and cries, and her mother responds, "You sound like a baby. Stop it." Jenifer's face gets red and she starts pounding her fists on the mattress. Jenifer's mother says, "Stop it now or you are going to lose your video game tomorrow." Jenifer screams, "You never loved me! You hate me, and I hate you. I hope you die!" Jenifer's mother gasps, "That is enough!" and slams the door on her way out. Jenifer screams, kicks, and throws things at the door for the next hour. Jenifer finally winds down a bit but sits next to the door and starts rocking back and forth and repeating, "I'm a bad kid, and everyone hates me." Jenifer's mother just wanted Jenifer to go to bed, but two hours later, they are both frustrated, angry, sad, and exhausted.

But how different that situation would turn out if Jenifer's mother followed *scenario #2:* Jenifer's mother starts the bedtime routine but notices something off with her daughter. "Jenifer, I notice that your body seems dysregulated. I can tell because you are using a different voice and you are rubbing your eyes. You seem anxious. Can you tell me about how you're feeling?" Jenifer doesn't have an answer and still refuses to comply with bedtime. "Jenifer, I can't let you stay up, but I can talk to you, rub your back, or tell you a story for five minutes—which would you like?" Jenifer begins to think about which she would like, distracting her from the original feeling of dysregulation. She insists that nothing is bothering her but asks her mom to rub her back anyway. Her body begins to relax as her mother rubs her back; she even opens up about some things that have been worrying her. Jenifer got in trouble earlier in the day at school when she was talking during class. She felt embarrassed. Then later, her friend didn't want to play with her on the playground. She tells her mother how sad she felt; those feelings came back to her as her body quiets down for bed. Jenifer asks her mom to tell her a short story. Jenifer's mom agrees. When the story was done, Jenifer tells her mom a little more about what happened. Her mom responds, "I'm sorry that happened. Do you know what I know about you? You are a good kid and you do great things. I love you." Jenifer is relaxed by then, and her mother is able to leave the room. It took an extra fifteen minutes but they both felt better and their bodies felt regulated.

Don't Give Up

It may take some time and consistency before you see positive results. Don't be discouraged. You may have to pull the car over several times and wait for thirty minutes while your child calms down before the day arrives where you can leave your house and drive straight to the park without interruption. It may take a long while before you can help your child find the words to accurately express their feelings without erupting into violence. Keep your head up, dear parent. We know how this feels. We have been there many times in the past. But we also know the transformational power of sticking with it.

What Now?

- Journal or talk with a friend:
  - What is a situation that you have concerns about with your child? What are some ways you could handle this situation differently in the future? Write out a plan or a script that you will use next time this situation occurs.
- Read our book *Honestly Adoption: Answers to 101 Questions about Adoption and Foster Care,* in which we answer the top 101 questions we receive almost every day. You will find everything from what to do when your teenager is still bedwetting to how to build healthy relationships with biological parents.

Remember . . .

- *One of our deepest needs as humans is to feel secure.*
- *Always come full circle with your child. Restoration is part of the attachment process.*

CHAPTER 15

COMMUNICATING WITH OTHERS

One July evening many years ago, I (Mike) was walking into our local youth camp's chapel to help lead a summer-camp session with the junior-high youth ministry I was leading at the time when my phone began vibrating. Kristin was calling and was in tears. "What's wrong?" I asked.

"We just returned home from our initial appointment with the new therapist," she said. "It was a disaster. She was condescending, rude, and kept asking our son if he was behaving badly because he has 'too many brothers.' Then she asked him if he wanted his 'real mom.'"

I was dumbfounded. We were so hopeful this new therapist would be the key to helping our son. "What did he say?" I asked.

"He looked at her with a confused look, then he looked at me. Finally he said to her, 'My mom's right over there, you big, fat dummy!' and pointed to me across the room. 'I see her every day, and I like my brothers!'" Kristin went on to tell me that the therapist interrupted her every time she tried to share or explain something about our family. And when Kristin tried to calm our son, who was getting increasingly agitated, she cut Kristin off with an accusatory tone, "Don't talk for him. He's a big boy, he can get himself calmed down."

Our son jumped up and yelled at the therapist. "Don't talk to my mom like that!" Kristin ended up carrying him screaming and flailing to the car while everyone in the office watched.

Perhaps you've been made to feel this way in a therapist's or pediatrician's office before. Maybe you've been talked over or made to feel stupid as you tried to explain some of the behavioral or health issues you were experiencing with your child. Perhaps you walked out of a provider's office feeling as if you were to blame for the struggles your child was having, and you received no help, no compassion, and no answers. It's frustrating. Beyond that, it feels hopeless.

You may have experienced the neighbor who gossips about your child, the pediatrician who downplays your concerns, or the teacher who doesn't want to compromise her classroom structure just for your child. Childhood trauma is invisible. Outsiders can't tell how your children are struggling and may further complicate the healing environment you are trying to provide. For years we have had teachers, coaches, small group leaders, even law enforcement say, "It doesn't look like anything's wrong!"

But you can successfully communicate your child's needs to others in a way that brings understanding, even partnership. Here's how to take your working knowledge of trauma, disrupted attachment, and behavior management and share it.

Teachers and School Administrators

It's always better for the school to hear from you with preemptive communication about your child than for you to hear from them with reactive communication. So communicate early and often.

When possible, contact the school before the school year starts. Set a time to meet the teacher when the classroom isn't crowded. Talk to the principal on the phone or introduce yourself over email. If your child has dietary needs, call food services. These aren't complex conversations, they're just an opportunity to introduce yourself. Contact your child's school at the first sign of a problem. I (Kristin) tend to let things fester too long because I don't want to bother the teacher. To my surprise, the issue is usually something that we could have solved with a quick phone call weeks earlier. Communicate often. We live in an age of instant communication—use it. Send your teacher a quick text to let them know of a change at home or send an email sharing a heads-up or asking a question.

There still may be times in which you'll have to deal with the school from a reactive standpoint. When you do, here's how you can arm yourself to get the best results.

Be Prepared!

Before you talk with your child's school, make sure you're ready. Research the laws in your area. Know what your state's schools are required to do, and what they are not required to do. Understand your rights and your child's rights in terms of what the school is required to provide for them. Gather ideas for possible classroom accommodations and testing that may be necessary, such as alternative-seating ideas within the classroom or modified schedules. Familiarize yourself with your child's teacher and administrators. And help them understand your child. You know your child the best. Imagine your child in the classroom. What challenges will they face? How does your child learn best? What helps your child stay focused? What might be a distraction? How will your child's history be a part of this particular classroom—for instance, will they be learning about genetics?

Create a Script

Decide ahead of time what you will need to share with your child's school. Who will you talk with and what information will you share? Condense all you want to say into bite-size pieces. Make yourself a copy of the laws and have it available to reference. Write notes and keep them handy when you are on the phone or in a face-to-face meeting. Practice, if you need to. Talk through your script with a trusted friend who has the ability to give honest feedback. Your friend can help you adjust your tone and language so you can communicate clearly when you are ready to talk face-to-face.

Stay Calm

You may feel the school should understand your child's history and their situation—especially in today's culture where these types of issues are becoming more familiar and prevalent. You may be frustrated because the school has failed to follow an accommodation that was listed in your child's 504 plan or IEP (Individualized Educational Plan). You may be justified. Now take a breath. Clear your mind before you approach the school with your concern. Put yourself in the shoes of the person you are communicating with and treat them the way you would want to be treated. Be calm and clear minded as you communicate with them.

Assume the Best

I (Kristin) want others to believe the best about me. I hope that when someone speaks with and about me it is with grace. Before speaking to the school, remind yourself to assume the best. These are professionals who care about education, their classroom, *and* your child. I am a principal's and teacher's kid. My grandparents, aunts, and uncles are all educators. Educators are real people. They have bad days and good. They have families, illnesses, celebrations, and a fantastic range of personalities. Get to know the people who are with your child every day and do your best to assume the best of them. Doing so will help you both grow a relationship that will benefit your child.

Lean on Your Support Network

If you need to take someone with you when you are talking with the school, lean on your support system. Often we can bring a therapist, family member, caseworker, pastor, or friend. Normally when we have gone this route in the past, we've notified the school that we are bringing our child's providers with us to meetings or conferences. The last thing we want to do is appear to be ganging up on our child's school.

Offer Solutions

Maybe your child is wiggling during story time or blurting out answers. Maybe your child is constantly crying just before recess. You may have some ideas about what to do. If possible, purchase resources, books for the classroom, fidgets, or special snacks your child can have. Your child's teacher will appreciate it.

Offer to help the teacher. Teachers have plenty of jobs they need help with in the classroom. Volunteer in the classroom, if you can. That might not be the best fit for your schedule or your child's personality, and that's okay. Offer to do what you can. You may be able to pick up extra supplies when you are out at the store or take papers home to cut for an upcoming craft. At our daughters' high school, we often volunteer to hold doors or stack chairs after special events. We both work from home, which gives us the advantage of flexibility. We can be door greeters at an open house for a few hours and take one more thing off the plate of the educators who spend so much time focused on our children.

Respect Your Child's Privacy

Not everyone in your child's life needs to know every detail. Share only what is necessary, because once you have shared your child's story, you cannot take it back. So tailor your communications to the audience. Ask yourself who needs to know what. And when you do share, kindly remind the person you're telling about privacy laws. Stress the importance of keeping your child's personal story private.

Several years ago, we had to attend an emergency IEP because our child was new to a school, and the guidance counselor and teacher of record wanted to learn more about his special needs. We went in prepared to give the basics of his diagnosis, but were careful not to overshare. In the process, we asked them to do the same if they are asked by other teachers or parents. Everyone in the room that day agreed, and we never had an issue.

Teach Your Child to Advocate

Our children won't be children forever, and they'll need to know how to do these things for themselves:

Teach them language. Teach your child the language around their diagnosis. Teach your child the language around their adoption. Talk about these things at home. Help your child decide what and who to tell about private information and practice how they will respond to a teacher or administrator or ask for help when you aren't there.

Model advocacy. Take your child with you whenever you can. Not all meetings at your child's school are okay for them to participate in, but some are. Allow them to listen in and encourage them to speak up. Afterward, you can talk with them about what happened in the meeting and what they learned about how to advocate for themselves.

Create opportunities to practice. Invite a trusted adult to practice with your child. You may encourage your child to spend the night at Grandma's house and have them advocate for themselves. They can talk to Grandma about what things help them fall asleep and what schedule they typically have at home. They can even negotiate one or two scoops of ice cream after dinner. Talk with the trusted adult ahead of time so they know how to encourage the child to work through these situations of advocacy in a positive way.

Law Enforcement

A child's diagnosis with something like FASD or autism may hinder your child's positive interaction with law enforcement. Your child may be nonverbal but may also be a good driver. They may be able to get a license but if they're stopped by law enforcement one day, their silence may be interpreted as disrespect. Think through the situations in which your child might face law enforcement. How might their diagnosis be a barrier for them? Here are ways to prepare your child and officers for any interactions they may have.

Prepare for Possible Scenarios

Think first about your child's previous interaction with law enforcement. Ask yourself: What is my child's experience with law enforcement? Was my child removed from his first mom and dad by an officer? Was my daughter interviewed by a police officer after her mother's death? Will my child run away if he sees a police officer? Will my child panic if she sees the lights of a police car? What will happen if an officer comes to my child's school? Thinking through the circumstances your child faced in the past will mark their experiences in the future.

Ask yourself: In what situations could my child come into contact with law enforcement? The resource officer at school, the police officer at a traffic stop, the security guard at the mall, or even the TSA agent at the airport could trigger a child who has had a past negative experience. A child who compulsively steals or is easily tricked into something may end up talking with law enforcement face-to-face. It seems odd to prepare for a child potentially having a run-in with the law, but we find it's better to be prepared than to be surprised. So as you prepare for possible scenarios, think too about possible responses. A child who runs away may experience contact with law enforcement who are trying to keep them safe. How will my child respond? Will my child panic, run, fight, cry, refuse to speak, admit to a crime they did not commit?

Ask yourself: Why will my child respond that way? What is it about my child's story or diagnosis that will cause them to respond to law enforcement this way? A child who refuses to talk may be afraid. A child who admits to a crime he did not commit may have an FASD. A child whose natural reaction is to fear may try to punch the officer.

The more you can prepare and help your child to prepare, the better the potential outcome.

How do we want or need our child to respond? If they are in contact with law enforcement, we need them to be calm, respectful, and focused. We need them to know where to find their identification and we need them to put their hands where the officer can see them, even if they are not in trouble. We need our child to answer the officer clearly. We need them to ask for a lawyer if he or she is being questioned. We need them to be clearheaded. Our children may respond out of their survival brain, in which case they will not be clear thinking, so we need to do some things to prepare them.

Prepare Your Child

It's important to talk to your child about law enforcement during times when there is no crisis. Practice how to behave at a traffic stop or when being questioned by an officer. Talk about their fears and worries. Discuss situations where they may find themselves in need of help or even in trouble. Practice what they will do in those situations. As three of our children, who are now teenagers, were nearing the preteen years, we walked them through scenarios where they may either encounter law enforcement or need to contact them. For instance, we explained to them what they should do, whom they should call, and what they need to say if there was ever an emergency situation (either health, weather, or behavior-related). Since these three, in particular, are African American, we walked them through how their tone, behavior, and attitude need to be if they are ever stopped by police for a traffic violation or otherwise.

Meet Law Enforcement

Set up a meeting to visit your local police station and fire station. Many towns also offer community activities that allow you to connect with local law enforcement, such as Coffee with a Cop (https://coffeewithacop.com/) or National Night Out (https://natw.org/about/). These events will acquaint your child with officers and first responders and recognize their faces. This will allow your child to see that most officers are there to help and not to harm. This will also give the officers an opportunity to get to know your family and your child. If there is ever a misunderstanding with your child, you want to have officers who know your entire family.

You will also want to prepare the police, just as you prepared the school by preemptively communicating with them. You may need to let the police or fire department know if your child has a diagnosis or medical condition that they need to know about. Get your child an ID bracelet, alerting professionals of any needed information. Some states are able to store this information in a computer system so when officers run a driver's license or address, they will know quickly that someone needs special assistance. If your child is a runner, you may be able to find resources from the police department to help locate the child in case of a crisis.

Police are the front line for mental-health emergencies. If your child is having a mental-health emergency, the police will probably arrive first. Prepare yourself and your child for this possibility. If you need help, ask for a crisis-intervention-trained officer. Explain clearly on the phone what your child's needs are and how the officer can help. You might say, "My child experienced extreme trauma as a child, and I need a crisis-intervention-trained officer. I need the car to arrive with no lights on. Please enter through the front door. I am unlocking it now. I am in the kitchen. My child is not armed. My child has a disability. I need help. My child is not a danger to the police." The more information you can give, the better.

Doctors and Therapists

While doctors and therapists are professionals, remember that you know your child and their needs best. You are the detective. You are with your child more than anyone. You are the connector between your child, their biological family, and the resources they need. Doctors and therapists need you to partner with them to give the best care and help to your child. Here's how.

Gather Information

Gather as much information as possible, including medical and family histories, etc. Anytime you can gather information, do it. Keep an accordion file for papers or scan them and keep a file on your computer. When you talk with a family member, you may find something out that you didn't previously know. Maybe Great Aunt Frida has diabetes. That information may not seem significant today but it may be a clue that will prove quite valuable in the future.

Prepare

Write down concerns and questions so you'll have them ready when you go to appointments or need to make emergency calls. Keep a notebook or use the note app on your phone. When you think of a question or concern, write it down right away. I (Mike) am terrible at forgetting things that I was sure I wasn't going to forget. Keeping a list of observations with me helps me to stay on track when I'm looking for good resources.

Keep a Log

Remember that log we encouraged you to use to keep track of behaviors? You can also use it to note medication concerns. This can be as simple as one or two words with a date and time, such as, "On this [date], after he took [medication], I noticed he seemed [specific behavior or observation]. Along with this, he was also participating in [activity] and this specific [season or life event] was also taking place." As you look over your notes, you may discover a concerning behavior started the same week as a new medication or an interaction with a new coach.

Respect Professionals

They spent years learning, and they deserve our respect. Not all professionals are good at what they do, this is true. When we approach others with an attitude of respect, however, we set the playing field to our advantage. Though they may not be the person we end up working with, we have done no harm by treating them respectfully. One of our values as parents has always been to show respect to professionals even if we don't care for their behaviors or methods, or were not treated in a respectful way by them. Why? Because our children are going to grow up and have to live, exist, function, and be an adult in this world someday. There is no better place for them to learn how to do this and how to respect others than from us. As it says in Proverbs 22:6, "Start children off on the way they should go, and even when they are old they will not turn from it." You and I have a responsibility to model respect for others in front of our children.

Consider Your Options

You do not have just one doctor or therapist to choose from, did you know that? Ask others, get recommendations, and do a Google search. Familiarize yourself with the professional before you even step foot in their office. Do your best if you are stuck. Sometimes we can't find a new podiatrist in our area because this is literally the only foot doctor for miles. But weigh your options. How often will you need to see this doctor? If it's only once or twice, you may need to make due with what you have. But if you'll need to interact with this doctor or therapist regularly, you want to make sure you and your child feel comfortable with them.

Before you choose a doctor or therapist, interview them. Ask about their experience with foster care or adoption. Ask about their experience with childhood trauma. Find out what they consider some of their successes. Ask about their knowledge of your child's diagnosis. Listen to their answers. Then when the interview is done, ask yourself if this person was willing to listen and learn. Were they open to learning and curious about your child? If not, it's time to move on.

Share Resources You Have with Professionals

When you are working with a professional, you can offer them resources too. You might find an interesting article that pertains to your child or their particular field of study. Share manageable-sized articles or books. If there is a conference in your area that you're planning to attend, invite them to join you. Connect them with other professionals who you know in an area they are interested in.

I (Kristin) have connected a few pediatricians with our local FASD clinic. It's amazing how many people didn't even know it existed.

Pastors, Coaches, and Club Leaders

For a long time, we didn't join any activities. No sports, no theater, no arts, no scouting. It was too difficult. Our children's behaviors were unpredictable and often left others either frustrated with us or with fodder to gossip about us. We found the latter hurtful and resigned ourselves to staying home. That worked for a while but it was lonely. What we finally learned is that rather than staying in isolation, we could change the outcome of many of these situations simply by preemptively communicating. The truth is that our children need community just as much as we do. So we can encourage them to get involved and help them learn how to connect with others.

If an activity captures your child's interest, let them get involved. It can provide opportunities for a widening circle of influence. Over time, your children may be able to build relationships with adults who will help them grow in character. When you are raising children who have come from such a vulnerable past, it can be daunting to step outside of the safety of your home. Take a deep breath. You can do this.

Get to Know the Organization

Ask around for recommendations before you join an activity. Read the handbook or visit the location and take a tour. Meet the director, pastor, coach, or scouting leader. Talk with them about who they are and why they like this particular organization. You'll learn a lot just by engaging in face-to-face conversation. You may find that a quick Google search will show photos of the activity or organization. You might see something there that causes you concern, such as a chaotic environment or a lack of diversity. Knowing this ahead of time may help you decide whether or not to participate, or it may give you a starting point to ask further questions.

Explore the environment. What will time spent with this organization look like? Take a trip to the organization and observe. Watch how the leaders interact with children and families. Visit during the time your child will be there. And find out how their activities are structured. What leaders are in charge? What does the schedule look like? How will your child respond to the personalities of those in charge? How will your child respond to the structure?

Ask if they are trauma informed. Some organizations will post their philosophy online or in their handbook. Many organizations are beginning to understand the need for trauma-informed care. This can mean a variety of things. Before you sign up and join in, ask the leaders what their experience is with childhood trauma, adoption, and foster care. Ask how they engage with children and families who have experienced trauma. Find out ways that they support foster and adoptive families. They may not have a plan and that's okay. If they are willing to learn and partner with you, the organization may be a healthy place for you to get involved.

Communicate with the Leaders

Spend time getting to know the leaders. What is the coach, club leader, youth or children's pastor like? Get to know them outside of the activity your child is involved in. They are real people; they have likes and dislikes and circumstances that may lead them to need support too. Getting to know simple things about the people who work with your child can be such a valuable relationship builder for your whole family. Knowing the youth pastor's favorite sports team or the soccer coach's favorite brand of soda can create a connection with them that will encourage them to have a better day, in turn helping them to be present and encouraging with your child.

Then share about your child. Remember, they do not need everything about your child's story. Decide what they need to know. If the child has difficulty with food insecurity, the soccer coach may not need to know but the camp director might need to. If your child acts out sexually, you may be able to supervise each baseball practice but you may need another adult to help with supervision, if your child joins a scouting troop. Most volunteers aren't bound by law to keep your child's information private. You will need to be careful who you share details with. If you do need to share something personal with a pastor, coach, or club leader, take some time to talk with them about the importance of privacy and the impact that sharing your child's private information with others could have on your child one day.

Prepare for Fun and Difficulty

I (Kristin) can be a glass-half-empty person sometimes. I would rather not do something if there is a potential risk. Thank goodness the rest of my family isn't like that. Consider best-case scenarios. How could this activity go well?

Be positive but also realistic. What are some things you anticipate might be difficult? Farm camp may be awesome for your active nine-year-old, but it might also be too long to be away from home. You might talk with the camp director ahead of time and let them know the potential challenges. Know the warning signs that this activity has become too much and plan for what to do if this happens. Once you decide to try an activity, prepare your child. Talk about what to expect. Ask if they have any questions and offer to take them to observe if possible. It's important to practice situations that may arise with the child. Practice what they will do if the coach or leader needs to correct them. Practice what they will do if they feel uncomfortable and need to use a coping skill. For instance, many years ago, when our oldest son was attending his first full week of summer camp, we drove there a few hours early to walk the campground so he was familiar with the area and would know his way around. We also reached out to the dean of his week of camp and asked if we could pair him up with a counselor who would be in his cabin and would also be his small-group leader throughout the week. Before the week started, we connected with this counselor and walked him through our son's diagnosis and some of his behavioral issues so this young man would be as prepared as possible. It ended up making the week very successful.

You'll also want to create an exit plan. What will you do if your child gets triggered? What will your child do? Practice the exit plan ahead of time. You might need to sit close by while your child gets adjusted to the environment. Then empower your child to create their own support. Talk with your child about what they will need to be successful at this activity. Are there any fidgets, snacks, or clothing that will make the child feel comfortable? What can they pack for themselves? What can they do to prepare for success?

Trust Your Child

Our children need to have ownership in what they do and how they navigate the world. Once we have done everything we can to prepare them and the adults around them, we need to step back and trust. Our very introverted daughter decided to audition for a musical when she was eleven years old. We were so nervous—what if she didn't make it? What if the other kids weren't friends with her? What if the adults didn't take time to get to know her? What if everyone misunderstood her shyness for snobbishness? We were exhausted and we weren't the one auditioning. When it came to the audition day, she was calm and collected. She stood before the directors and about one hundred parents and students. Then she belted out the most beautiful and powerful song we had ever heard. The crowd gasped in astonishment that something like that could come out of such a meek little thing. She knew though. If we wouldn't have trusted her instinct and preparedness, she would have missed an incredible way to use her talent.

Trusting them doesn't mean you can't still be involved. Offer support whenever you can. Volunteer to assist or buy supplies and snacks. Support the organization by offering solutions where needed to help keep your child regulated and successful. Offer resources if possible for further learning about your child, his or her diagnosis, or general understanding of trauma. Offer resources that will support the entire team, class, or group. And then let the fun begin!

Extended Family Members

Family is such a valuable and complicated thing. We desire to live at peace with our family above all else. Most of us dream about warm family gatherings and joyous holiday dinners. While we can't let our dreams hinder our sense of reality, we also need to make sure that a relationship with family members is healthy for our child. We may need to adjust our expectations of extended family relationships and we may need to ask our family to adjust their expectations of our child. These healthy relationships will begin first with careful communication. When it comes to relationships like these, as well as relationships with any professional or provider, we lean heavily on the words of the apostle Paul in Romans 12:18: "As far as it depends on you, live at peace with everyone." What I (Mike) love about this particular verse is that we are only responsible for ourselves. We are not responsible for other people's behaviors or reactions. So with extended family, for example, we must approach them with as much peace and camaraderie as possible. It's up to us to do this. In the process, we need to be open to walking them through the basic understandings of our children's special needs, or diagnosis, and why they may behave the way they do in certain situations. However, if we determine that our family members are not going to be supportive, or even do damage through words or actions, we may need to set up strong boundaries, or even distance ourselves from them. Our children's well-being, as well as our family's well-being, comes first.

Consider What the Relationship Might Look Like

Ask yourself what relationship you can reasonably expect between your child and your family. How will this relationship affect everyone involved? What struggles might arise with family? Do you have a family member who will not understand your child? Is it possible that someone in your family will not respect your child or the way you parent? What will that dynamic look like? You know your family and you know what your child is walking into when you have a family gathering. Be realistic with your expectations so that you can respond appropriately and respectfully to all involved. That will also help you set boundaries with respect.

Be respectful and polite. It is possible to set boundaries in a respectful way. Remember, you may be the only example of adoption or foster care they see. Also remember that your children are watching how you treat others and they will model their relationships after yours.

Create a Script

Just as you created a script before engaging with school personnel, so too you can create a script for your child to engage with family members. Decide ahead of time what information you and your child are willing and comfortable to share. Practice what your child might say if a family member asks about something you and your child are uncomfortable with. The script might be, "I don't feel comfortable talking about that," or "You'll need to ask my mom about that."

Creating a script empowers our children to set boundaries for themselves. Having a script handy when interacting with others will give them the power to take ownership over themselves and their story.

Set Boundaries

We must set boundaries even with family members. It is okay and necessary to set boundaries around your child's story to protect your child's privacy. Your extended family should not know anything about your child that the child doesn't already know. If a family member is asking a question that is too personal, set a clear boundary. Be respectful and firm.

If you have a family member who is unkind to your child, stick up for your child. You have an obligation to your child before others. You may face criticism from family members who do not understand why you do what you do. If you can help them understand, you will gain a partner. But if they do not support you, you may need to say, "I know you don't understand why I parent the way I do, but I need you to support me or I need you to give me space."

It's also important to set boundaries around your time and environment. You may need to communicate before an event to let everyone know what will be healthy for your family. For instance, you may need to set a time limit for your visit. You may need to stay in a hotel during the holiday season so your family can have a place to regroup. You may need to create an exit plan or you may need to decline altogether. If you have some family members who understand what is going on, and what your family needs, sit down with them and have a conversation ahead of time so they know you do not intend to hurt anyone's feelings; this is just something you need to do to stay healthy for now.

Invite Them to Learn More

Invite a trusted family member to know and understand a little more about your child. Ask them to support you and your child at family functions by helping the child use supports and coping skills. This family member can be an ambassador to the rest of the family by helping shape positive conversations around adoption, foster care, and understanding of trauma.

You can test the water with them by asking your family, "Would you like to know more about how trauma changes the brain?" You may be surprised to find that they are interested, and with knowledge will come understanding. As you introduce the subject of trauma, keep your examples vague. You may want to point out that everyone experiences trauma and help your family member understand trauma from their own experiences. Specifically, if your child has a diagnosis (such as an FASD), you could say they experienced trauma before birth, but not get into specific details about behaviors or triggers.

—————————— **What Now?** ——————————

- Journal or discuss with a friend:
  - ○ List some of your past experiences with professionals. What happened specifically? What did you do or say that you now know you could have done differently?
  - ○ As you set up new consultations with providers, what are some key things you need to communicate?
  - ○ Who are members of your extended family you need to reach out to and have a heart-to-heart with about your child's circumstances and/or trauma history?

Remember . . .

- *You are the connector between your child and the professionals who will offer them needed resources.*
- *You set the tone for family relationships. Your children are watching.*
- *You are the connector between your child and the world around them. You can offer the keys to help your child one day be able to participate on their own.*

CHAPTER 16

PARENTING YOUR CHILDREN INTO ADULTHOOD

When I (Kristin) first started parenting, I thought my children would have a life of clear direction and ease. I believed if I raised them in the church, they would always make wise choices, pursue healthy relationships, and live at peace. I think I got that idea from the verse we just shared in the previous chapter, "Start children off on the way they should go, and even when they are old they will not turn from it." You can imagine my surprise when it turned out that my children are human just like me! A wise friend once told me, "Proverbs 22:6 says, 'When they are *old,* they will not turn from it.'" Her adult children went through significant trauma in their early lives and their paths have been anything but straight. Through their preteen and teenaged years, their extreme behaviors led to arrests, expulsion, neighborhood fights, running away, the list goes on and on. Yet she refuses to lose hope for them. She is assured, however, that they are learning and growing throughout their lives—just as we all are. Most importantly, she has not stopped pursuing them and working to build a secure attachment with them, even though several still push her away when she attempts to help them, and even try to manipulate her into giving them money or bailing them out.

When we lay a foundation of trust, love, kindness, healing, respect, and faith for our children, they will return to that foundation one day. Mind you, this could be a long journey. Working to rebuild broken attachment can take years. But it is possible.

Your parent-to-child relationship may look very different from that of other parents. You may be involved in ways your parents weren't involved in your life. Your child may continue to live with you beyond childhood because they need your care and connection. It can also be difficult to watch other parents' children mature and take on independence as adults while your children still require more hands-on parenting from you.

No matter how old or young your child is, now is the time for you to begin considering what your parenting role may look like after childhood so both of you can be more prepared.

Your New and Continuing Roles

Over the course of two summers, more than two decades ago, our parents individually watched the two of us graduate high school in separate towns. A few months later, they packed up cars and moved us into college. Mine (Mike) took place in the summer of 1995, and Kristin's took place the following summer in 1996. As each set of parents drove away from our college campus, they shed tears, they felt sadness, but they also celebrated. They each drove home confident that we would succeed, that we would be okay, that we could make it on our own, with minimal guidance, and no supervision necessary. Occasionally, we would each call home and ask for advice or just catch up with our parents as friends, as adults do. Our parents didn't need to manage our bank accounts, keep a daily medicine log, or walk into a professor's office to help us advocate for a grade change or any special assistance the two of us needed. We were on our own. Growing up in a typical fashion, free of chronic trauma, with two sets of caregivers who nurtured each of us, and had a secure attachment with each of us, allowed us to step into the world and become independent. Our secure attachment means that we can call our parents when we need help while confidently maintaining our independence.

However, many of our children will not trust their attachment with us even into adulthood and may continue to push away even when they need help. We will have to show up and continue to build trust and secure attachments in ways our parents never had to. But what does that look like specifically when you're parenting your children into adulthood?

Active Caregiver

As your child is growing up, you are hands on (perhaps even vigilant). The fact is, your role may not change all that much from what you are currently providing, or you may continue to be hands on, involved in medical or therapeutic care, involved in crucial decision making, even managing your child's bank account, bill payments, and more. If you find yourself needing to assist your child long term, it can feel overwhelming. Being an active caregiver may mean your child lives with you past high school. Often adult children will need to live at or near home into adulthood in order to benefit from the assistance of parents. Fortunately, many services are available today that aid caregivers in continued care of their children. In Indiana we have a program called BDDS (Bureau of Developmental Disabilities Services),[1] which provides services for adults living with disabilities, such as transportation to and from a job, mentors who can help balance a bank account or pay bills, and even continued medical care. While this doesn't necessarily mean parents are uninvolved, it does serve as a companion to caregivers who are actively involved in caring for adult children. To find out what services are available in your area, do a Google search for "Developmental Disability Services."

Advocate

Your child may be self-sufficient and able to function in society with less help from you but they have an uphill battle. This is the child who, as a young adult, lives in her own apartment, can get herself up on time for work, get out the door on time, and be productive at work but has trouble remembering to pay her electric bill, or quickly spends all her paycheck and then realizes she doesn't have money for food. Or she may be independent but blows through relationships and can't understand why people are frustrated with her and never call her back. You will have opportunities to step in and become a voice for them and next to them as they climb this mountain of a world that does not lend them any favors. Your role may change from active caregiver to advocate. You may have the opportunity to coach them as they advocate for themselves. You may still be a vital part of their experiences at a medical provider's office, at work, with finances, and with navigating relationships. You will be constantly handing them bite-size responsibilities.

Supporter

The role of supporter places us in a position that is quite different from the role we hold as parents of young children. Our main role as a supporter is to listen and stand beside our children.

This can take on several different aspects. For instance, you may help them find and move into their first apartment. You may be asked to babysit once a week for your grandchildren. As a supporter, you may be called on to help your child talk through a problem they faced with a coworker. You will be there to celebrate college graduation, new jobs, marriage, and grandchildren. You may attend doctor appointments or community activities with your child as an extra set of listening ears and nothing more.

The role of supporter may also be one you take if your child faces natural consequences for choices they make or extreme behaviors they have. This could include serving prison time, losing a job, losing friends, being evicted, or losing transportation. In the unfortunate case that any of these circumstances happen, you will most likely be completely powerless to do anything or to change their circumstances. But you can encourage them. You can stand by them when they walk through the darkness of natural consequences.

Friend

Secure attachments will help build a solid foundation for your child to live a healthy, independent life. The opposite side of hands-on parenting with your child into adulthood is the transition into friendship. We are experiencing this with our eldest daughter who is now in her thirties. She and her husband and children (our grandchildren) frequently visit with us, spend time during the holidays with us, and show up for birthday celebrations at our house. We have even spent time out on the town and at social gatherings with her. This was not a major facet of our relationship when she was a teenager. In those years, she needed parental guidance. Now we have a beautiful adult-to-adult relationship.

You can take heart in knowing that, regardless of the struggles you may go through when your child is in the early childhood or adolescent phases of growing up, there's still hope to have a solid friendship with them when they are older. Secure attachments can lead to friendship.[2]

Mentor

Finally, you may not have to walk hand in hand with your child when they are an adult, but you may be the person they seek out for advice or insight into the complexities of life. Remember, regardless of maturity levels and personal development, your child may still wrestle over and certainly contend with their trauma history and attachment issues. They can heal from it, but it's still a part of their story. They may need you to be a phone call or text away to discuss critical situations or challenges in order to formulate how they respond to them.

Carol and her husband, Shawn, adopted baby Claire at birth in 1994. Claire grew up healthy and happy. Claire struggled with a feeling of loss and abandonment throughout her life, but her parents stayed close and supported her through her self-discovery and healing. When Claire went to college, there was rarely a day that passed where she didn't call her mother to vent, ask advice, or share recent news from college. When she graduated from college and eventually got married, she and her mother talked nearly every day. They had moved past a caregiver/child relationship and into a mentor/mentee relationship.

At times, each of these stages of parenting adults can and will overlap. You can be a hands-on parent and a friend in the same day.

Setting Up for Your Child's Successful Adulthood

One of our children is nearing his eighteenth birthday and close to moving out on his own. We are certain he will need services well into his adult life, perhaps even throughout his entire life. Seeking resources, having next-step conversations, and planning for adequate care when he's an adult did not start in the past year or even two years. In fact, the planning started when he was in sixth grade. Even before your child reaches adulthood (if you haven't already crossed into this phase), you need to line up the proper resources he will need to succeed in the second phase of his life. No matter the age, whether early childhood, preteen, or teenage, you can begin this process. Not only will finding them other sources help them to succeed, it will also significantly lighten your load as a parent. Here are two helpful starting points:

Get an Official Diagnosis

Success begins with a proper diagnosis. If you suspect your child may have been drug and alcohol exposed in utero (or you know there was a history of drug and alcohol abuse with their first parents), or you are witnessing certain behaviors or characteristics that mirror something you know could be a possibility with your child, such as high anxiety, inability to stop their body from moving, lack of impulse control, rapidly developing agitated behaviors, inability to focus or care for themselves properly, lack of executive functioning skills, to name a few, it's crucial that you seek out professionals who can provide the diagnosis. If your child has a mental illness or medical diagnosis, do your best to find out that diagnosis during childhood. The label may seem scary, but the diagnosis can open doors to supports that may make all the difference in gaining your child's self-sufficiency. With an official diagnosis, your child can receive more services than we can provide on our own. For instance, an official diagnosis will allow your child access to an IEP, a specific strategy for accommodations for a student to help them be successful in their education. This plan travels with them through elementary, middle, and high schools, and even into college. These are legal plans that must be followed by educators and administrators.

As we mentioned earlier, the Bureau of Developmental Disability Services is a perfect place to find support for your adult child. If you're wondering what this looks like in real time, we recently worked with a couple who noticed their nineteen-year-old daughter's behaviors had begun to escalate and often rendered her with an inability to focus, or even function properly throughout a day. This had started happening a few years before, but by the time she had reached sixteen years old, the behaviors were severe. So severe, in fact, that she nearly flunked out of the high school she had just started attending. At their wits' end, they reached out to their local pediatrician, who had cared for their daughter through her entire childhood. She recommended they contact the genetics department at a large children's hospital in the city they lived in. They did, and soon had an appointment set up to see a specialist within the genetics department who provided an official diagnosis of ARND (alcohol-related neurodevelopmental disorder under the umbrella of fetal alcohol spectrum disorders). Through receiving an official diagnosis, they were able to set up an IEP at her school (remember, IEPs can follow your child into their college careers). With added assistance, she began to do much better in school. While an official diagnosis may seem daunting, scary, or even confirmation of a disorder, they are necessary for providing your child with the care they need to succeed in life.

Save Documentation

Save any documentation you can find—from medical records to personal histories. Save your child's case files from foster care or their adoption. Save any paperwork connected to their biological family. Keep reports from school, doctors, and psychiatrists. Keep a file of contact information for any specialists your child works with. You will need to pass these things on to your child as they grow. You may also need to access these documents if you need to advocate for your child in adulthood.

Every year, we take manila file folders and write each of our children's names on them, and we keep a file folder on the desktop of our computer with each child's name. We have done this since they were born (or entered our family). In those folders we save everything. And we do mean everything. Every email, every mail correspondence, every handwritten note from a doctor, therapist, or case manager, every IEP report (you get the idea). We go to Office Depot before the year begins and purchase an accordion-type file holder and label them with the year we are currently in. We can go back to any year of our children's lives with us and pull out any documentation we may need, or a provider may need. When it comes to saving documentation, there is never too much detail or any amount of going overboard.

Your Role during the Transition Period

You need to prepare yourself and your child for an adequate transitional period between them being a child who needs being parented and a young adult who is gaining independence. We've already talked in previous chapters about the importance of having these conversations beginning when your child is in the preteen or adolescent stage, but it's equally important that you make sure the transition from home into young adulthood is as smooth as possible. Nothing should be abrupt or fast-ending. If your child ends high school and does not feel prepared to enter college or to live on his or her own just yet, take your time. Don't rush it. Likewise, well before the end of high school, start involving your child in life experiences and teaching them life skills.

Think about the life skills they need as an adult. If you weren't available to do something for them, what would they need to be able to successfully handle on their own? These are the things you need to help them navigate before they become adults. These life skills include understanding the value of money. Work with them over a period of time to form and manage their own budget. You can teach them how to use budgeting software and stay hands-on with them for a season until they've learned to do it on their own.

Also, give them opportunities to speak for themselves. Mike and I do not go into our children's interviews when they apply for jobs, nor do we even call in their prescriptions to the pharmacist (when they're teenagers). They have been given the power to do this on their own. Of course, we keep track of their progress, but we release them to make these decisions and phone calls. Let your children begin to make their own appointments and allow them to express themselves without relying on you to do it for them when they are in with their pediatrician or therapist, when they are in an IEP meeting, or when they are with an employer.

Teach them to manage their medications. Help your child set up a system that will help them remember which medications to take and when. This can be an alarm, photos of the medications, or a weekly pill box with times and doses written on them.

Watching Your Child Deal with Rejection

Ed and Sherrie have stood by, helplessly, and watched as their daughter has been rejected over and over. "We know she misses social cues every now and then but, man, she's such a fun-loving kid and she really does love others genuinely. So hard to watch!" Ed confessed, as tears welled up in his eyes. She's a beautiful young woman. She makes good grades, and is a dedicated softball player. She often deals with anxiety and doesn't easily understand boundaries with others. While she never does anything inappropriate, she can quickly become overbearing with her friends, or resort to immature behavior. Thus, she is often rejected by fellow students or players on her team. "It's a heartbreaking and crushing feeling," Sherrie told me (Mike).

For some of our children, the damage to their original attachments have caused misunderstandings about relationships throughout life. Social cues can feel abstract and confusing and so can issues of trust. Friendships and family relationships can be more difficult for our children. As our children step into adulthood, they will begin navigating these relationships without the buffer we once created.

When you learn that your child is struggling with rejection in some way, remember that your role has shifted to supporter. The best thing you can do is be available for them and listen. Be open to hear what happened without giving advice or interrupting. Do not pass judgment about the situation. This isn't your story and this isn't your experience. Your child may need to talk or grieve or be mad or stay silent. Stand by while they work through their feelings. Just because they are now adults doesn't mean that they don't still need your encouragement and to feel your love. So pursue them. Call, text, visit, and invite your child into a relationship with you. When they are feeling the sting of rejection, it may bring up feelings of their childhood trauma. Do your best to let them know they are not alone. You can encourage them to see their therapist, if they have stopped going. You can also encourage them to pray and seek a spiritual outlet, knowing they are never truly alone in a relationship with God.

Dealing with Rejection *from* Your Child

Several years ago, one of our children planned a birthday party with some of her close school friends. We promised to provide snacks, decorations, and a movie for them to watch. On the day of the party, we spent several hours cleaning the house, making special treats, and then driving into town to rent her favorite movie from Blockbuster Video (yep, this happened a long time ago). When it came time for the party, we noticed she'd placed all of our snacks in a separate room away from the gathering, and then proceeded to place all of the snacks her friends brought out for selection. Later on, we noticed the movie we rented for her was still on the kitchen table. When we went downstairs, they were watching a different movie that one of her friends brought. Though this type of rejection wasn't blatant, it still hurt. Because of the trauma she went through in her early years, she had an inability to trust what we said we were going to do. She hadn't believed that we would provide for her the way we said we would. She often pursued care from other people, or she would attempt to provide for herself.

Your adult child may reject you. They may boldly tell you they don't want a relationship or they may simply stop answering the phone. Don't lose hope. Parenting is different with adults, but your job isn't over. Your child may be experiencing cognitive delays due to exposure to trauma or prenatal substance exposure. They may be experiencing delays due to their initial disrupted attachment. They may be experiencing some of the desire to push away that they should have felt during the developmental stages of adolescence. Similar to our child, your child may not trust that you are going to be there for her, or that your home is his or her forever home.

With maturity comes new understandings and more complex questioning. Our adult children will begin to push away from us and try things on their own. That is natural and good. As they grow, they may face new questions about their identity, their trauma experiences, and their place in the world. This can be especially complicated for children who have been adopted or spent time in foster care. Even if our children may push us away during this time, we must maintain a delicate balance of staying connected and allowing them to have space. How do we do that?

We continue to love and support them even if they push us away or refuse our help. This may be hard to deal with, especially if we were hands-on in caring for them through their childhood and adolescence. Remind them that the front door of our house is always open, the phone line is always connected, and we aren't going anywhere, regardless of what they are going through.

We must remember that their rejection of us is because they are still dealing with their issues and their identity. Our adult children are learning who they are and where they fit in the world. They may meet biological family members for the first time. They may be navigating parts of their culture of origin that they aren't familiar with. Ideally, we have been celebrating their unique identity throughout their childhood. As they grow older, their rejection of us may be because we are safe, because we happen to be the person who is strong enough to handle the trauma they are still navigating. So even when they reject us, that doesn't mean that we respond in like ways. We need to be the firm foundation they can count on. We need to show that they are undeniably a part of our family as well as wholly a part of their biological family.

Keep in touch with them as much as you can. Invite them for holidays, family gatherings, or birthday parties, even if they don't respond or haven't shown up in quite some time. You may want to put their Christmas presents aside and pull them out when they arrive so their absence doesn't overshadow the celebration with the children who are there. Remember, your child's brain has been altered by trauma. They have a hard time seeing the world as safe, or healthy, and that may include you. That's why you must take the lead in demonstrating grace and acceptance.

Continue to Encourage Healing

Even though your role and relationship with your children will change as they move into young adulthood, you still have the opportunity to help your child experience continued healing. Three of our children are now in their adult years and we have not stopped pursuing relationships with them, or working to build a secure attachment with them. We recognize that healing and restoration could take a lifetime. Thus, even though they are on their own, some raising their own families, we pursue healing. Trauma and attachment issues don't disappear once a child turns eighteen or once a child moves out, gets an apartment, and begins to live independently. They will still need you to help them navigate and process those issues, especially because you've been the constant who has walked through the dark times with them and have proven your trustworthiness. Nothing brings healing or restoration like an open ear and an open heart. Let your child know that you are invested in helping them continue to heal and to set them up for success as they enter the future. Then you can pursue their healing through these other avenues:

Connect Your Children to Adult Adoptees

Your children need people they can share with who just get it. This connection is vital. They need to have people to look up to who have gone down this road before them. Even though you've walked the road with them, you haven't been in their "shoes." That's where connecting with other adult adoptees can bring them strength and clarity. They will face questions about identity, adoption, race, and faith that they will not always want to discuss with you. They need a community that belongs to them. Help your child find a community of adoptees. There are many adult adoptees who have stepped into the online space and are providing valuable, transformational content that helps us parent better.[3]

Connect Your Child to Counselors Who Understand Trauma

Your child may not have the same counselor in adulthood that they had in childhood. However, a good experience with a counselor will set them on the right track to seek help in the future if and when they need it. They should know to ask for a counselor who is trauma trained. They should seek out a counselor who is experienced in the specific issues related to foster care and adoption. Teach your children to interview any counselor they are considering and impress on them that it is their right not to work with any professional who makes them uncomfortable.

Care for Your Own Heart

It's okay that this feels hard. As your children transition to adulthood, your role is a little less certain too. Care for yourself. Allow yourself to spend time with friends. Nurture a new hobby. Take a break. Be gentle with your heart. As your child struggles through parts of this transition, it's okay to feel sad, worried, and even a little lost. Give yourself some grace.

Now What?

- Journal or talk with a friend:
  - What stage of parenting are you in with your child? If your child is still at home, what do you need to do now to help them prepare for adulthood? If your child is grown, what are some ways you are still connecting and building trust with them now?
  - What are some trust-building things you can do starting today?

Remember . . .

- *You are raising an adult. Everything you do in childhood is in preparation for them to become an adult.*
- *If your child is an adult and you still do not have a secure attachment, do not give up hope. You still have time.*
- *Pursue your adult child, even your child that pushes you away.*
- *Don't lose hope. None of us grow up overnight. You and your child will figure this out.*

CHAPTER 17

BELIEVING
FOR MORE

We hope you have been encouraged by what we've shared and that you have the resources you need to parent differently. Maybe you have arrived at this point feeling hopeless or even a bit lost. You may still find it difficult to see past the storm you are currently in. You've logged hundreds of thousands of hours fighting for this child, advocating for better services, traipsing all over creation because the only provider who takes Medicaid is on the opposite end of the city or county. We have been on this journey for nearly two decades now and we still walk through seasons like this. The biggest truth you need to believe in is that there is hope. Hope comes through the discovery that you are not alone.

As part of the support group we attended in 2011, each week we sat in a room with seven other couples who were parenting children with major trauma histories. We listened to their stories. We processed with them their struggles and fears. Our hearts collectively broke for one another. We learned better parenting strategies, and for the first time, we felt hopeful that we could parent our children into healing and secure attachment. We returned to our home rejuvenated and armed with knowledge and wisdom. Though our children weren't miraculously healed—and neither were we— we *were* and are stronger knowing that we aren't alone.

Healing from trauma and securely attaching isn't something that happens quickly. It takes time and investment, and even as you begin applying what you've learned in this book, you may not see immediate results, but that's okay. You're on the road toward healing. You've taken important first steps. Don't give up! The sun is still shining for you and your family.

Healing Is Possible!

In June 2015, I (Mike) spent a week in San Diego speaking at a leadership conference for high school students. The time there was enriching, fulfilling, and encouraging, not to mention that we experienced the most perfect weather in the world. As wonderful as it was, by the week's end, I was ready to head home and kiss my babies. A week away from Kristin and my children was too much, and I was more than eager to board my plane heading back home to Indiana.

My flight connection was through Denver, which is notorious, especially in the spring and early summer, for having terrible storms move through the area. This day was no different. We landed in Denver under some intense circumstances—lightning, thunder, and a torrential downpour. One by one, every departing flight became delayed. I watched my 4:00 p.m. departure move to 5:00 p.m., then 6:00 p.m., and finally 7:45 p.m. With each delay, I became more frustrated. *I just want to go home and see my family*, I thought. No, actually, this was something I was screaming in my mind. Every time the thunder clapped and lightning flashed, I seethed inside. In the middle of my desperation and frustration with my current circumstances, all I could see around me was this massive storm. It had enveloped the entire terminal.

At 7:15, we finally started to board the plane bound for Indianapolis. By 7:45, we were taxiing to the runway—all the while being rocked back and forth by the wind and rain. With every jerk and sway, I found myself feeling more and more hopeless. *They're going to delay us again.* I began to believe that the storm would never end, and I would never get home.

We began rumbling down the runway for takeoff, and after a few more jerks and whips back and forth, our plane lifted into the dark gray and threatening-looking sky. The plane shook and swayed. I wasn't afraid; I was too busy feeling angry about missing the kids' bedtime. As I was lost in thought, something bright caught my eye. It was coming from outside the plane. I could see only a bit of it because my window shade was pulled halfway down. I raised the shade, ready to peer into the stormy sky, but the storm had now vanished. We had risen above the storm and now bright light was coming from the most beautiful sunset I had ever seen. Below were the dark gray clouds and the flashes of lightning from the storm we had just moved out of.

When we were on the ground, we couldn't see this light or sunset. The sun had never ceased to exist; the storm was just covering it. Storms are only temporary. The sun's light is constant.

When you find yourself in a storm, be it the constant battle with providers or your child's school or extended family, be it struggles to get them to listen to you, or even fighting against your child's behaviors that you cannot figure out how to stop, remember, this is only temporary. This is a storm. The sun is still shining for you and your family. The light is still covering the earth around you. It's still bringing warmth that a storm can never provide.

Your child's trauma history is not the end of their story. Their trauma history does not define their future. You cannot base their future life on their present seven-, eight-, nine-, or fifteen-year-old behavior. Remember, healing is possible. That's the hope we hold for our children. We believe in the same personal transformation and restoration for our children as we do for ourselves. We believe in a God who can and will bring beauty from the storms of this life. Regardless of the darkness we've experienced, we believe there is light, there is healing.

Keep Working toward the More

You know by now that your parenting will not end the moment your child turns eighteen. That's a good thing, because you get to take advantage of even more time to build a trusting relationship with your children. For a lot of us, our children will need to build secure attachments with us well into their adult years. You can take hope in the fact that time is on your side here. You have a lifetime to change, and to grow and heal with your children. But what does this look like as it relates to building a secure attachment with your child? Let's explore this more in-depth.

You Have More Relationship to Build

I (Kristin) went through years of feeling guilt and shame before I understood our child's trauma. I felt as though I had done irreparable damage to my children by reacting in ignorance to what was really going on with them. Then after years of doing things the wrong way, I learned how to parent more effectively through gaining valuable knowledge on how our children's trauma history impacts their present-day behaviors. As soon as I realized that, I started working toward mending our relationship and providing a foundation for healing, trust, and security. It's never too late to learn, grow, and heal with our children. Each of us can start today to make the changes that are necessary for secure attachments.

You Have More Memories to Make

While we may have entered into our children's lives late in the game (two of ours came to us when they were teenagers), we can begin today creating memories as a family that they will carry with them forever. Some of our favorite memories are of volunteering for our daughter's high school choir competition, taking our grand-kids to the zoo, and sharing long conversations over steaming cups of coffee with our grown children. We used to panic that we were running out of time to build relationships, but now we know that the time we spend building trust with our older children is just as valuable as the attachments we formed with our younger children.

Your Child—and You—Have More Healing

When we reframe our understanding of our child's behavior through the lens of compassion, we open up a world of healing. And healing allows for more secure attachments and healthier life choices and relationships. You have a chance to heal and help your child heal. If you've made a million mistakes, as we have, you can start fresh today. You have so much more healing you can pursue between you and your child. Start by apologizing to your child for your failed understanding or misguided parenting. You may say something like, "I'm sorry I reacted so strongly when you didn't come to Christmas dinner last year; I was hurt. I didn't realize how you were feeling about Christmas. Thank you for telling me how much your mother used to love Christmas and how much you miss her at this time of year. What can we do differently next year to celebrate this special day in a way that honors your mother and leaves room for your grief?"

You and Your Child Have More Grace to Give and Receive

We all get a fresh start because of grace. For us, grace means receiving something good that we do not deserve. As people of faith, we believe that we gain a chance at holiness because Jesus died to pay the price for our sins. Because our past mistakes have been wiped clean by this undeserved gift, we are prompted to do the same for others. As parents, it is our joy to see grace played out as we position ourselves in a place of understanding instead of correction and punishment. As Christ has forgiven us the mistakes we make in our humanity, so can we forgive the behaviors our children display, which are born out of past trauma. In this forgiveness and extension of grace we find we are able to connect with our children in a way that is trusting, predictable, secure, and made for healing. When we extend this grace, and understanding to our children, we are also more likely to extend it to ourselves, forgiving ourselves for not being perfect and allowing ourselves to move forward in a way that is filled with compassion for our children and for our family.

Secure Attachments Are Possible

Your journey is not over. This is just the beginning. Each time you gain a deeper understanding of your child, you lay a brick on the foundation of your attachment. Each time you respond to your child with patience and grace, you are building your foundation stronger. Each time you strengthen yourself as a parent, you are sealing the foundation with wisdom. Dear parent, we wish you the best as you move forward. We believe in you, we believe in your family, and we hope you will find peace as you and your child become securely attached.

ACKNOWLEDGMENTS

There are literally thousands of people to thank with this book. Where do we even begin?

First and foremost, we both want to thank our parents, brothers, and sisters for supporting every spontaneous, risky, wild adventure we've ever jumped into. From racing our bikes down the steps of Grandma's house (Kristin) to auditioning for and landing a role in a play without any previous acting experience (Mike). From becoming parents to eight children to leaving our jobs to write full time. You have never stopped believing in us, and for that, we are grateful.

To our eight beautiful children—you have taught us so much about life, compassion, love, and hope. We are better human beings because of you. Thank you for your patience as we strive to be better parents each day. We love you all so much!

To our best friends in the world, John, Nicole, Ryan, and Megan, we are who we are because of your support and love. Here's to another twenty, or thirty, or hundred years together!

To our hardworking team at The Honestly Adoption Company. You are the best in the land. Thank you for believing in this dream and embracing the mission. The way you love families is inspiring.

To the parents who strive each day to parent well, we stand beside you. This book is for you!

NOTES

Chapter 1: Everyone Experiences Trauma

1. Bessel Van Der Kolk, *The Body Keeps the Score* (New York: Penguin, 2014), 21.
2. Nancy Newton Verrier, *The Primal Wound: Understanding the Adopted Child* (Baltimore: Gateway Press, 1993, 2016), 1.

Chapter 2: Trauma and the Brain

1. William C. Shiel Jr., "Medical Definition of Brain Stem," MedicineNet, December 4, 2018, https://www.medicinenet.com/script/main/art.asp?articlekey=2517.
2. "Know Your Brain: Amygdala," *Neuroscientifically Challenged*, June 24, 2014, https://www.neuroscientificallychallenged.com/blog/know-your-brain-amygdala?rq=amygdala%20limbic.
3. Dr. Karyn Purvis teaches on this concept, "Attachment as a House," through Empowered to Connect parent training sessions, https://thewholehouse.org/etc-parent-training-2-3/.

Chapter 3: Resiliency and Healing

1. Darcia Narvaez, "Believing 'Children Are Resilient' May Be a Fantasy," *Psychology Today*, June 13, 2011, https://www.psychologytoday.com/intl/blog/moral-landscapes/201106/believing-children-are-resilient-may-be-fantasy?amp.
2. Michael Unger, *Counseling in Challenging Contexts* (Belmont, CA: Brooks/Cole Cengage Learning, 2010), 14.
3. Bessel Van Der Kolk, *The Body Keeps the Score* (New York: Penguin, 2015), 212.

Chapter 4: Attachment and Healing

1. Bessel Van Der Kolk, *The Body Keeps the Score* (New York: Penguin, 2015), 212.
2. "Sex Trafficking," National Foster Youth Institute, https://www.nfyi.org/issues/sex-trafficking.

Chapter 5: How Trauma Disrupts Attachment

1. Nancy Newton Verrier, *The Primal Wound* (Baltimore: Gateway Press, 2016), 20–21.
2. Karyn Purvis, *The Connected Child: Bring Hope and Healing to Your Adoptive Family* (New York: McGraw Hill, 2007), 50.

3. Verrier, *Primal Wound,* 90.
4. Verrier, *Primal Wound,* 21.

Chapter 6: Building the Foundation for Healthy Attachments

1. Karyn Purvis, *The Connected Child* (New York: McGraw Hill, 2007), 51.
2. Karyn Purvis, Empowered to Connect Simulcast, 2015, empoweredtoconnect .org.

Chapter 8: Is It Bad Behavior or Something Else?

1. Joyce Cooper-Kahn and Laurie Dietzel, "What Is Executive Functioning?," Learning Disabilities Online, http://www.ldonline.org/article/29122/.

Chapter 11: Managing Crisis Behavior

1. Karyn B. Purvis, David R. Cross, Donald F. Dansereau, and Sheri R. Parris, "Trust-Based Relational Intervention (TBRI): A Systemic Approach to Complex Developmental Trauma," National Center for Biotechnology Information, October 2013, https://www.ncbi.nlm.nih.gov/pmc/articles/ PMC3877861/.

Chapter 12: Emotional Regulation and Self-Care for the Caregiver

1. As Dr. Kristen Neff points out in *Self Compassion: The Proven Power of Being Kind to Yourself.*
2. "Dialectical Behavior Therapy," *Psychology Today,* https://www.psychology today.com/us/therapy-types/dialectical-behavior-therapy.
3. Mike Berry, *Confessions of an Adoptive Parent: Hope and Help from the Trenches of Foster Care and Adoption* (Euguene, OR: Harvest House, 2017), 146–48.

Chapter 16: Parenting Your Children into Adulthood

1. Bureau of Developmental Disabilities Services, Family and Social Services Administration, https://www.in.gov/fssa/ddrs/2639.htm.
2. For more ways to leverage your influence now to see massive relational dividends when your child becomes an adult, see Mike Berry, *Winning the Heart of Your Child: Nine Keys to Building a Positive Lifelong Relationship with Your Kids.*
3. We encourage you to follow us on Instagram @confessionsofaparent to learn more.

ABOUT THE AUTHORS

Mike and Kristin Berry are authors, bloggers, speakers, parent coaches, adoptive parents, and former foster parents. They are passionate about reaching adoptive and foster parents around the globe with a message of hope and transformation. They are the creators of the award-winning blog website *Confessions of an Adoptive Parent* (recently changed to *Honestly Adoption*), which has a global audience of more than 150,000 people every month, and the award-winning podcast *The Honestly Adoption Podcast*, which receives more than 20,000 downloads every month. Kristin is the author of three books including *Born Broken: An Adoptive Journey*, *Honestly Adoption: Answers to 101 Questions about Adoption and Foster Care* (coauthored with Mike), and *Keep the Doors Open: A Year in the Life of a Foster Parent*. Mike is the author of four books, including *Confessions of an Adoptive Parent: Hope and Help from the Trenches of Foster Care and Adoption*, *Winning the Heart of Your Child: 9 Keys to Building a Positive Lifelong Relationship with Your Kids*, *Replanted: Faith-Based Support for Foster and Adoptive Families* (coauthored with Josh and Jenn Hook), and *Honestly Adoption: Answers to 101 Questions about Adoption and Foster Care* (coauthored with Kristin). They have been married for twenty-one years and have eight children, all of whom are adopted. They live on a farm in Indiana.

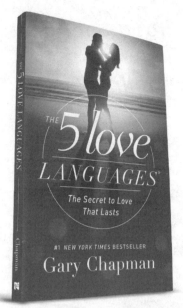

Discover the secret that has transformed millions of relationships worldwide. Whether your relationship is flourishing or failing, Dr. Gary Chapman's proven approach to showing and receiving love will help you experience deeper and richer levels of intimacy with your partner—starting today.

978-0-8024-1270-6

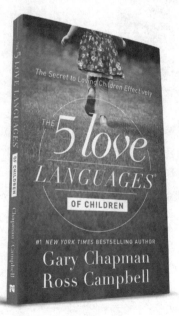

Two family relationships experts help you discover your child's primary love language and how to speak it. Once you learn how to convey love, affection, and commitment in ways that resonate specifically with your child, you will see so much improve, including your child's emotions, behavior, confidence, and relationship with you.

978-0-8024-1285-0

also available as eBook and audiobook

NORTHFIELD
PUBLISHING

Quiet the voices of "not good enough"
and step courageously into
guilt-free homeschooling

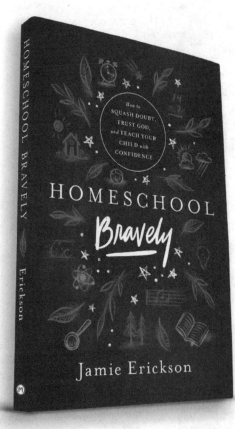